DISASTER MANAGEMENT

MSWE-03

Notes For

Master in Social Work [MSW]

Useful For

IGNOU, KSOU (Karnataka), Bihar University (Muzaffarpur), Nalanda University, Jamia Millia Islamia, Vardhman Mahaveer Open University (Kota), Uttarakhand Open University, Kurukshetra University, Seva Sadan's College of Education (Maharashtra), Lalit Narayan Mithila University, Andhra University, Pt. Sunderlal Sharma (Open) University (Bilaspur), Annamalai University, Bangalore University, Bharathiar University, Bharathidasan University, HP University, Centre for distance and open learning, Kakatiya University (Andhra Pradesh), KOU (Rajasthan), MPBOU (MP), MDU (Haryana), Punjab University, Tamilnadu Open University, Sri Padmavati Mahila Visvavidyalayam (Andhra Pradesh), Sri Venkateswara University (Andhra Pradesh), UCSDE (Kerala), University of Jammu, YCMOU, Rajasthan University, UPRTOU, Kalyani University, Banaras Hindu University (BHU) and all other Indian Universities.

GullyBaba Publishing House Pvt. Ltd.

ISO 9001 & ISO 14001 CERTIFIED CO.

Regd. Office:
2525/193, 1st Floor, Onkar Nagar-A,
Tri Nagar, Delhi-110035
(From Kanhaiya Nagar Metro Station Towards Old Bus Stand)
Call: 9991112299, 9312235086
WhatsApp: 9350849407

Branch Office:
1A/2A, 20, Hari Sadan,
Ansari Road, Daryaganj,
New Delhi-110002
Ph.011-45794768
Call & WhatsApp:
8130521616,8130511234

E-mail: hello@gullybaba.com, **Website**: GullyBaba.com

New Edition

Author: Gullybaba.com Panel

Copyright© with Publisher

All rights are reserved. No part of this publication may be reproduced or stored in a retrieval system or transmitted in any form or by any means; electronic, mechanical, photocopying, recording or otherwise, without the written permission of the copyright holder.

Disclaimer

Although the author and publisher have made every effort to ensure that the information in this notes is correct, the author and publisher do not assume and hereby disclaim any liability to any party for any loss, damage, or disruption caused by errors or omissions, whether such errors or omissions result from negligence, accident, or any other cause.

If you find any kind of error, please let us know and get reward and or the new notes free of cost.

The notes is based on IGNOU syllabus. This is only a sample. The notes/author/publisher does not impose any guarantee or claim for full marks or to be passed in exam. You are advised only to understand the contents with the help of this notes and answer in your words.

All disputes with respect to this publication shall be subject to the jurisdiction of the Courts, Tribunals and Forums of New Delhi, India only.

About Publisher

Gullybaba Publishing House is the brainchild of Mr Dinesh Verma, his name alone evokes profound respect and admiration. He is the pioneer of providing quality materials to the students of IGNOU because, having been a student of IGNOU, he understood the difficulty and pain of the non-availability of quality materials himself. He is serving the students with the following services:

EXAM-SUCCESS GUIDES

Important questions, solved question papers, guess papers - all in one! to score good marks in lesser time and effort.

FREE BOOK

As our love and care for our students, here is a Free Gift – A Famous Book "Secrets to Pass IGNOU Exams with Less Study" for you. You can download it now! https://www.gullybaba.com/ignou-free/

YOUR CONTRIBUTION TO MOTHER-EARTH

When you read our books, you save our mother earth as we use recycled paper to make these books. On every purchase, we contribute something to plant a plant.

SOLVED ASSIGNMENTS PDFs / HAND-WRITTEN

Best and genuine solved assignments PDFs you can instantly download from Gullybaba.com or our App.

PROJECT REPORTS/SYNOPSIS

Best Quality No-Rejection projects/synopsis by professionals researchers in ready to refer format.

MOBILE APP

You can download 'Gullybaba' app from Google Play Store to enjoy all above services at one place.

Why Gullybaba's IGNOU Help Books

Is Fear of Exams making you stressful? Are you not getting good marks in your IGNOU exams? Are you looking for sure-shot solution get ahead in your IGNOU studies? Look no further than the answer: Gullybaba.com! With our expertly crafted course help-books, you'll be ready to face any exam with ease-guaranteed. What's more, we offer a huge discount on IGNOU Help Books Combo Deals – Save BIG.

Now, complete IGNOU courses more quickly and with Good Marks in Lesser Time & Effort.

Home Delivery of GPH Books

You can order Gullybaba Books online from Gullybaba.com or Gullybaba App. We dispatch books on the same day of receiving the order through our fastest courier partners.
You can also order books through WhatsApp on 9350849407 or by email at order@gullybaba.com.
We also provide "Cash On Delivery" through our courier partners and sometimes Govt. Postal Department.

Important Note to Sellers

Selling this book on any online platform like Amazon, Flipkart, Shopclues, Rediff, etc. without prior written permission of the publisher is prohibited and hence any sales by the SELLER will be termed as ILLEGAL SALE of GPH Books which will attract strict legal action against the offender.

Notable Information

An attempt has been carefully made to present this book more useful and meet the requirement and challenges of the course prescribed by IGNOU University. We hope that this effort will fulfil the readers' expectations and help them excel in exams. Referring to University study material alongside this book is like "icing on the cake".

We wish you a successful and rewarding career. If you have any feedback to improve our books/products, please email at feedback@gullybaba.com. Because we believe, "Feedback is breakfast of champions" and our readers are our strength.

Table of Contents

Question Papers

Chapter-1

Introduction to Disaster Management

Q1. Write short note on the followings:

(i) Hazard

Ans. A dangerous phenomenon, substance, human activity or condition that may cause loss of life, injury or other health impacts, property damage, loss of livelihoods and services, social and economic disruption, or environmental damage. There are two types of hazards, namely:

- **Natural:** These are hazards caused by nature such as floods, droughts, earthquake, cyclones, tsunami, landslides etc.
- **Human made:** These are hazards that are caused by human beings either deliberately or by accident such as industrial and chemical accident, road and railway accidents, aviation disasters, fire, building collapse, communal violence, bomb blasts etc.

The High Powered Committee on Disaster management that was constituted in August 1999 under the chairmanship of Shri J.C. Pant identified five major groups of hazards in its final report. This exhaustive classification of over hazards is as follows:

Group (1): Water and Climate related Hazards

- Floods and Drainage Management
- Cyclones
- Tornadoes and Hurricanes
- Hailstorm

- Cloud Burst
- Heat Wave and Cold Wave
- Snow Avalanches
- Droughts
- Sea Erosion
- Thunder and Lightning

Group (2): Geologically related Hazards

- Landslides and Mudflows
- Earthquakes
- Dam Failures/Dam Bursts
- Mine Fires

Group (3): Chemical, Industrial and Nuclear Hazards

- Chemical and Industrial Disasters
- Nuclear Disasters

Group (4): Accident related Hazards

- Forest Fires
- Urban Fires
- Mine Flooding
- Oil Spill
- Major Building Collapse
- Serial Bomb Blasts
- Festival related disasters
- Electrical Disasters and Fires
- Air, Road and Rail Accidents
- Boat Capsizing
- Village Fires

Group (5): Biologically related Hazards

- Biological Disasters and Epidemics
- Pest Attacks
- Cattle Epidemics
- Food Poisoning

(ii) Vulnerability

Ans. Vulnerability describes the characteristics and circumstances of a community, system or asset that make it susceptible to the damaging effects of a hazard. Vulnerability can be defined as the diminished capacity of an individual or group to anticipate, cope with, resist and recover from the impact of a natural or man-made hazard. The concept is relative and dynamic. Vulnerability is most often associated with poverty, but it can also arise when people are isolated, insecure and defenceless in the face of risk, shock or stress.

People differ in their exposure to risk as a result of their social group, gender, ethnic or other identity, age and other factors. Vulnerability may also vary in its forms: poverty, for example, may mean that housing is unable to withstand an earthquake or a hurricane, or lack of preparedness may result in a slower response to a disaster, leading to greater loss of life or prolonged suffering.

Vulnerability can be of varied types like:

(1) Physical Vulnerability may be determined by aspects such as population density levels, remoteness of a settlement, the site, design and materials used for critical infrastructure and for housing (UNISDR).

Example: Wooden homes are less likely to collapse in an earthquake, but are more vulnerable to fire.

(2) Social Vulnerability refers to the inability of people, organizations and societies to withstand adverse impacts to hazards due to characteristics inherent in social interactions, institutions and systems of cultural values. It is linked to the level of well being of individuals, communities and society. It includes aspects related to levels of literacy and education, the existence of peace and security, access to basic human rights, systems of good governance, social equity, positive traditional values, customs and ideological beliefs and overall collective organizational systems (UNISDR).

Example: When flooding occurs some citizens, such as children, elderly and differently-able, may be unable to protect themselves or evacuate if necessary.

(3) Economic Vulnerability: The level of vulnerability is highly dependent upon the economic status of individuals, communities and nations The poor are usually more vulnerable to disasters because they lack the resources to build sturdy structures and put other engineering measures in place to protect themselves from being negatively impacted by disasters.

Example: Poorer families may live in squatter settlements because they cannot afford to live in safer (more expensive) areas.

(4) Environmental Vulnerability. Natural resource depletion and resource degradation are key aspects of environmental vulnerability.

Example: Wetlands, such as the Caroni Swamp, are sensitive to increasing salinity from sea water, and pollution from stormwater runoff containing agricultural chemicals, eroded soils, etc.

(iii) Disaster

Ans. A disaster is a serious disruption, occurring over a relatively short time, of the functioning of a community or a society involving widespread human, material, economic or environmental loss and impacts, which exceeds the ability of the affected community or society to cope using its own resources. In contemporary academia, disasters are seen as the consequence of inappropriately managed risk. These risks are the product of a combination of both hazards and vulnerability. Hazards that strike in areas with low vulnerability will never become disasters, as in the case of uninhabited regions.

A natural disaster is a natural process or phenomenon that may cause loss of life, injury or other health impacts, property damage, loss of livelihoods and services, social and economic disruption, or environmental damage.

Various phenomena like earthquakes, landslides, volcanic eruptions, floods, hurricanes, tornadoes, blizzards, tsunamis, and cyclones are all natural hazards that kill thousands of people and destroy billions of dollars of habitat and property each year. However, the rapid growth of the world's population and its increased concentration often in hazardous environments has escalated both the frequency and severity of disasters. With the tropical climate and unstable land forms, coupled with deforestation, unplanned growth proliferation, non-engineered constructions which make the disaster-prone areas more vulnerable, tardy communication, and poor or no budgetary allocation for disaster prevention, developing countries suffer more or less chronically from natural disasters. Examples include stampedes, fires, transport accidents, industrial accidents, oil spills and nuclear explosions/radiation. War and deliberate attacks may also be put in this category. As with natural hazards, man-made hazards are events that have not happened—for instance, terrorism. Man-made disasters are examples of specific cases where man-made hazards have become reality in an event.

(iv) Capacity

Ans. Capacity is sometimes described as the opposite of vulnerability, but this overlooks the fact that even poor and vulnerable people have capacities. Indeed, the starting point for capacity development is the existing knowledge, strengths, attributes and resources individuals, organizations or society has. Capacity may include infrastructure, institutions, human knowledge and skills, and collective attributes such as social relationships, leadership and management.

Some examples of capacity are:

- Permanent houses
- Adequate food and income sources
- Fire stations
- Developed health infrastructure,
- Good Community Network for support
- Local knowledge
- Strong community leadership and organizations

Capacity = 1/Vulnerability

(v) Risk

Ans. Risk is the possibility of losing something of value. Values (such as physical health, social status, emotional well-being, or financial wealth) can be gained or lost when taking risk resulting from a given action or inaction, foreseen or unforeseen (planned or not planned). Risk can also be defined as the intentional interaction with uncertainty. Uncertainty is a potential, unpredictable, and uncontrollable outcome; risk is a consequence of action taken in spite of uncertainty. Risk perception is the subjective judgment people make about the severity and probability of a risk, and may vary person to person. Any human Endeavour carries some risk, but some are much riskier than others.

Risk is a function of hazard occurrence and the projected losses. A societal element is said to be 'at risk' or vulnerable when it is exposed to hazards and is likely to be adversely affected by the impact of those hazards if and when they occur, especially in situations of limited capacity.

It can be best explained by

$$\text{Disaster Risk} = \frac{\text{Hazard} \times \text{Vulnerability}}{\text{Capacity}}$$

The relationship between these four components, indicate that each of the three variables that define risk- the hazard, the elements exposed and their vulnerability - are of equal value. Reducing any one or more of the three contributing variables will lessen the risk to a community. In reality, however, there is little opportunity to reduce the hazard component, therefore, only the vulnerability and the elements at risk will vary. When hazard and vulnerability are high, it will cause disaster but when capacity is present, it will decrease the impact, Hence, to reduce the risk of a disaster,

- Decrease the vulnerability of the community; and
- Increased the capacity of the community.

(vi) Relationship between hazard, vulnerability and disaster:

Ans. A disaster happens when a hazard impacts on a vulnerable population and causes damage, casualities and disruption. An earthquake in an uninhabited desert cannot be considered a disaster, no matter how strong the intensity might be. An earthquake is disastrous when it affects people, infrastructure and activities.

- hazard × vulnerability = disaster

  when extent of hazard and vulnerability is low, the resulting disaster will also be small magnitude.
- HAZARD × vulnerability = disaster

  When extent of hazard is high but vulnerability is low then the disaster will be of small magnitude.
- Hazard × VULNERABILITY = disaster

  When vulnerability is high but extent of hazard is small then the resulting disaster will also be of small magnitude.
- HAZARD × VULNERABILITY = DISASTER

  When extent of hazard is very high and the vulnerability is also high then it will result in a huge disaster.

Q2. Explain briefly the "Disaster crunch model".

Or

Elaborate the disaster pressure and release model.

Ans. The disaster Crunch Model states that a disaster happens only when a hazard affects vulnerable people. We can therefore see that vulnerability - a pressure that is rooted in socio-economic and political processes - is built up and has to be addressed, or released, to reduce the risk of a disaster.

A disaster happens when these two elements come together. A natural phenomenon by itself is not a disaster; similarly, a population maybe vulnerable for many years, yet without the "trigger event", there is no disaster.

A cause of disaster is hazard which is the '*trigger event*'. It could be an earthquake, landslide, floods, communal violence etc. The '*unsafe conditions*' are the vulnerable context where people and property are exposed to the risk of disaster. Vulnerable physical environment and unstable economy are some of the factors influencing these conditions.

The '*dynamic pressures*' within the society are the immediate cases of 'Unsafe Conditions'. They are the processes and activities that have translated the effects of root causes into unsafe conditions.

Beneath the dynamic pressure are the '*underlying causes*' which make the community and structure to be unsafe and vulnerable. They are the basic fundamentals or ideologies on which society is built. Vulnerability develops from a progression of underlying conditions to dynamic pressures and finally creating unsafe conditions.

Disaster Pressure and Release Model: the Pressure and Release Model (PAR Model) is a model that helps understand risk in terms of vulnerability analysis in specific hazard situations. PAR is a tool that shows how disasters occur when natural hazards affect vulnerable people. The vulnerability of people is rooted in social processes and underlying causes which may be isolated from the disaster. The foundation of the PAR model is that a disaster is the connecting factor between two opposing forces. The two opposing forces are what generate vulnerability and the natural hazard event. The release part of the model considers the reduction of the disaster. To relieve pressure, vulnerability has to be reduced.

Disaster Crunch Model helps us to understand how vulnerability is built up whereas the Disaster Release Model helps us to understand how the risk of disaster can be reduced.

The first stage is to examine the disaster event itself. Natural phenomena cannot be prevented but their risk of getting out of control and causing damage and loss of life can be reduced. Measures can be undertaken to modify or reduce the hazards. For example, to reduce the risk of river flooding, protective dikes or bunds can be built and the system of river control can be linked to flood warning systems. If 'unsafe conditions' are to be turned into 'safe conditions', then it is necessary to adopt activities, which will lessen the 'dynamic pressures'. For Example, Mitigation measure for an earthquake prone area can include providing incentives to encourage the community to strengthen their homes, to vacate particularly dangerous house locations or to build new houses in a safe manner to resist local hazards.

The next step is to reduce pressure that directly or indirectly contribute to the growth of vulnerability. For an earthquake prone area, the basic developmental activities can be undertaken to significantly reduce lives lost or damage to property for future disasters.

Introduction of disaster preparedness plans:

- Building or strengthening of local institutions.
- Education of local builders and masons.
- Initiation of income generating activities.

Q3. Describe the followings:

(i) Hazard Assessment

Ans. A hazard assessment is the process used to identify, assess, and control workplace hazards and the risks to worker health and safety. The assessment is an essential part of an organization's safety culture and safety management system. The hazard assessment should begin with the identification of what natural hazards can be expected and how they might change in the short and medium term as a result of climate change. First of all, all of the potential hazards are identified. Then the areas that could be affected by the hazard are marked, this is called Hazard Mapping. The magnitude, intensity and frequency of the hazards are determined and the causes of the hazards are investigated. Hazards could include earthquakes, volcanic eruptions, floods, drought, cyclones and epidemics.

Hazard analysis refers to prioritizing disasters based on its frequency and analysis of the estimated losses. This can be carried out by taking the help of elderly people of the village. The community can analyze the losses that they had incurred during various disasters and learn the best practices carried out. This is an important activity as it forms the basis for preparedness and mitigation plans.

The community can be asked to review and analyze the occurrence of past disasters and hazards. Group discussions along with the elderly population, teachers and children can be held focusing on the disasters and hazards faced by the community for the past one year to past fifteen years, kind and nature of disasters and hazards faced, experience in the last hazard faced, warning issued, damage caused, response to the disaster, relief and rehabilitation process, traditional methods of coping of the community, gaps in management of the hazard, lessons learnt. It can be useful in understanding the nature, intensity and behavior of the past disasters and hazards. The elderly population can share vital information and experience about the past while the presence of children in the group discussion can ensure that the experience is passed on to the next generation.

Tools for Hazard Analysis: Some of the tools that can be used for hazard analysis are as follows:

(1) Hazard Mapping: Hazard mapping is a form of worker participation that concerns marking hazards at work stations on a map. Hazard mapping can be applied to various issues, such as work safety, working with chemicals, exposure to noise etc. It is a visual representation of the village by the community. It is a rough spatial overview and sketch of the area and specific locations, which are vulnerable to various hazards. The main feature of hazard mapping is to facilitate discussion on issues pertinent to hazards. It is made by men and women, who know the area and are willing to share their experiences on large sheets.

(2) Historical Profile or Timeline: This tool is used to gather information about what happened in the past. It helps in getting an insight in past hazards, changes in their nature, intensity and behaviour. It helps to understand the present situation in the community and establish the link between hazards and vulnerabilities. The community may also become aware of the changes that have taken place over the past through historical profile or timeline.

(3) Seasonal Calendar: It involves making a calendar showing different events primarily the time of occurrence of hazards throughout the annual cycle. It helps to identify the periods of stress and prepare for the specific stress in and prepare for the specific stress in normal times before the threat of hazard looms large on the community. The facilitator can arrange sessions for the community members focusing on the issue.

Hazard	J	F	M	A	M	J	J	A	S	O	N	D
Flood												
Drought												
Epidemic												
Any Other												

(4) Hazard Matrix: This tool aims at gathering comprehensive information about the past hazards. It helps in having an insight about the future hazards on the basis of gaps and lacunae in the management of past hazards and disasters.

Hazard	Intensity	Early Warning Given or not	Warning sign	Speed of onset	Frequency	Time	Duration	Impact
Flood								
Earthquake								
Drought								
Industrial Hazard								
Epidemic								
Any Other								

(ii) Vulnerability and Capacity assessment

Ans. Vulnerability and Capacity Assessment (VCA) uses various participatory tools to gauge people's exposure to and capacity to resist natural hazards. It is an integral part of disaster preparedness and contributes to the creation of community-based disaster preparedness programmes at the rural and urban grass-roots level.

VCA enables local priorities to be identified and appropriate action taken to reduce disaster risk and assists in the design and development of programmes that are mutually supportive and responsive to the needs of the people most closely concerned.

The first step of vulnerability and capacity assessment is to record the actual impact of the hazard on elements in the five categories. Different hazards will affect these categories in different ways. For example, a flood may have a very large impact on houses (physical) and livelihoods (economic), but perhaps a much smaller impact on the forest and fish (natural resources). On the other hand, a drought may have a big effect on the natural resources, but a very minor impact on physical infrastructure. In the question sets, the first question in each category is always to do with the impact of the hazard. A participatory tool (e.g. a map, seasonal calendar or timeline) will help to define the impact more clearly and to identify vulnerabilities and capacities. Remember that in the individual category, impact on men and women may not be the same. When the impact on particular elements is high, the vulnerabilities which allow this impact must be identified. This is done by asking a number of 'why' questions. If the impact on particular elements is low, these elements are likely to become the capacities which enable a family or community to withstand and recover from the hazard.

Tools for Vulnerability Assessment: The various tools for vulnerability analysis are as follows:

(1) Transect Walk: This can be used to get a better understanding of the environment of the community at risk and provides a chance to inquire and assess physical/material vulnerability

The process involves taking a systematic Walk with key informants through the community to explore spatial differences, land use zones by observing, asking, listening, informal interviews and producing a transect diagram.

(2) Problem Tree: This tool can be used to show the relationships between vulnerabilities and enables the community to express the priority vulnerabilities which the local government should address first. The trunk represents the problems, the root depict the causes while the leaves signify the effects.

(3) Livelihood Analysis: The tool focuses on the studying the vulnerability of the livelihood of the community to various disasters. The tool analyzes the various livelihood activities that are spread over the year and the impact of hazards on the livelihood activities. It also focuses on understanding livelihood strategies, behaviour, decisions and perceptions of risk, capacities and vulnerabilities from different socio-economic background.

(4) Vulnerability Assessment: The vulnerability assessment would focus on the vulnerable community and the vulnerable infrastructure. It assesses and maps the more vulnerable population and the assets of the community.

Capacity Assessment focuses on identifying locally available assets and resources that can be utilized for building the capacities of the community during and after disasters. The local community has a lot of inbuilt strength and capacity for handling the disasters. It is important to capture the capacity and strength of the community in resource analysis. Apart from infrastructure and funds, it could be individuals with specific skills, local institutions and people's knowledge as all these have the capacity to create awareness and bring about changes in the community. Capacity Assessment, is therefore, not limited to a map depicting the available resources but also plotting of the distribution, access and its use by taking into consideration prevailing sensitiveness within the community.

The process would involve identifying safe houses and buildings for shelter, strong buildings, elevated uplands and structures, safe evacuation routes, health, medical and sanitation facilities, swimmers, doctors, nurses, sources of funds to carry out preparedness activities, volunteers for task force etc.

Tool for Capacity Assessment: One of the tools that can be used for capacity assessment is as follows:

Social and Institutions Analysis: The tool focuses on identifying various government, non-government and private organizations working in the field of disaster management in the local as well as neighbouring area. Various other aspects can also be studied such as the role played by the institutions, their area of interest, their importance in the management of disasters, capabilities of such institutions and the perceptions people have about them.

(iii) Risk assessment

Ans. Disaster risk assessment is a process to determine the nature and extent of such risk, by analyzing hazards and evaluating existing conditions of vulnerability that together could potentially harm exposed people, property, services, livelihoods and the environment on which they depend. In this way, informed decisions can be made regarding steps to reduce the impacts of disasters.

A comprehensive risk assessment not only evaluates the magnitude and likelihood of potential losses in case of a disaster but also provides full understanding of the causes and impact of those losses. DRA is an integral part of the decision making process. It therefore needs to engage multi-stakeholders from various disciplines and requires close cooperation and collaboration of different organizations and institutions of the target area.

(1) Risk Identification: Risk identification includes activities like hazard data collection and mapping to determine the frequency, magnitude and location of any hazard event; vulnerability assessment of the populations and the assets exposed and risk assessment to determine the probability of expected losses.

(2) Risk Reduction/Mitigation: It consists of measures taken to reduce the physical, social and environmental vulnerability and have been achieved through a number of ongoing schemes on resource conservation and management like Integrated Wasteland Development Program (IWDP), Drought Prone Area Program (DPP), Flood Control Programs, National A-forestation and Eco Development Program (NA and ED), Accelerated Rural Water Supply Program (ARWSP), Crop Insurance, and Mahatma Gandhi National Rural Employment Guarantee Yojana (MGNREGY) etc. Mitigation measures may include structural and non-structural measures like construction of cyclone/temporary shelters; plantation of mangroves and coastal forests along the coast line as these fall under the non-structural mitigation measures; construction of location specific sea walls and coral reefs in consultation with experts; development of break waters along the coast to provide necessary cushion against cyclone and tsunami hazards; development of tsunami, cyclone detection, forecasting and warning dissemination centers etc.

(3) Risk Transfer: Policies that govern the relief expenditure are based on the recommendations of successive financial commissions. The Calamity Relief Fund (CRF) and the National Calamity Contingency Fund (NCCF) were two main sources for meeting the relief expenses. Added to these are funds from international or multilateral donor agencies like World Bank, USAID and International and National/Local NGOs for relief and rehabilitation measures apart from government policies on risk insurance and micro-finance and micro-credit schemes.

(4) Early Warning and Forecasting: There are two distinct types of tsunami warning system- the International tsunami warning systems, and Regional warning systems to detect hazards like cyclones and tsunamis and to issue warning to reduce the loss of life and property.

Tool for Risk Assessment: One of the tools that can be used for risk analysis is as follows:

Risk Analysis: The tool is based on determining the risk by analyzing the vulnerabilities and capacities of the community related to each hazard. On the basis of analysis the risk is determined for a particular hazard in a ranking order. While conducting the risk assessment one should keep the following points in mind:

- Determine the risk by ranking.
- Ask the community about the hazard which poses the highest risk.
- Explore the reasons due to which a particular hazard poses the risk.

Q4. Describe the different perspectives on disaster.

Ans. Disasters affect populations, simultaneously creating public health and behavioral health challenges for the impacted communities. When disaster strikes, physical consequences–damage, destruction, disruption, displacement, death, debility, and disability–are most often overt and observable. Disaster public health needs are starkly evident.

The literature on disasters offers several definitions from different perspectives as summarized in the following heads:

- **The magnitude of the Damage Produced by the Event:** Human losses, number of injured persons, material and economic losses and the harm produced to the environment are often considered in order to define a disaster. For some like Dombrowsky (1998) the number of 25 deceased has to be exceeded; for others like Sheehan (1969) this figure has to be higher, more than 100 deceased and more than 100 injured or losses worth more than one million US dollars; or even higher Tobin (1997) an event leading to 500 deaths or 10 million US dollars in damages. According to Wright (1997) experience shows that when an event affects more than 120 persons, except for cases of war, non-routine interventions and coordination between different organizations are needed something which is already pointing out another important characteristic of a disaster. For German insurance for example damages greater than one million marks or more than 1000 deceased are needed, these figures are obviously given in order to limit responsibilities of insurance policies. To define a disaster by the magnitude of the damage caused however has many inconveniences. First, it may be difficult to evaluate the damages, especially in the initial stages. Second, such definitions are of no use for comparative studies in different countries or social situations and are affected by inflation, Dynes (1998). Third, disasters have a different impact in different environments: an earthquake of intensity may cause fright in Japan but may be a catastrophe in case of India or any other developing country.

- **Exceptional External Agent:** Disasters are often considered as events from the physical environment which are harmful for human beings and are caused by forces which are unfamiliar to them. Disasters are normally unforeseen and catch the populations and administrations affected off-guard. However, there are disasters that repeat themselves, for example in areas affected by flooding and others which are persistent, as in many forms of terrorism.

  Disasters are normally considered as events that occur "by chance" and therefore unavoidable. In the past they were ascribed to divine punishment, and even nowadays it is not unusual to read that an event '"'reached Biblical proportions', or that nature's powers have been unchained as they were when God had to punish the evildoing of human beings with the Flood. In fact, the etymology of disaster, from Latin (dis "lack" or "'ill-", astrum "heavenly body", "star"), indicates bad luck or fortune.

  An important characteristic of disasters is their centrality. H@h Cata- strophes are disasters of a great centrality. A total breakdown of everyday functioning takes place in them, with the disappearance of normal social functioning, loss of immediate leaderships, and the insufficiency of the health and emergency systems, in such a way that the survivors do not know where to go to receive help.

- **The Nature of the Agent:** In disaster produced by the inclemency of nature, the kind of disaster normally determines the way the pain is perceived and the quantum of guilt. Some more foreseeable, as for example in hurricane areas, volcano eruptions or floodings, and others are not so foreseeable, as in some earthquakes or massive fires.

- **Threat to the Social System:** United Nations Coordinating Committee for Disasters (UNDRCO, 1984) stipulates that a disaster, seen from a sociological point of view, is an event located in time and space, producing conditions under which the continuity of the structures and of the social processes becomes problematic. The American College of Emergency Medicine (ACEM, 1985) points out that a disaster is a massive and speedy disproportion between hostile elements of any kind and the available survival resources.

  The same appears in a definition by the World Health Organisation: 'A disaster is a severe psychological and psycho-social disruption that largely exceeds the ability to cope of the affected community'

  Disasters are event affecting a social group which produce such material and human losses that the resources of the community are overwhelmed and, therefore, the usual social mechanisms to cope with emergencies are insufficient.

  Therefore, three levels of disasters have been described:

  Level I (a localized event with victims; with local health resources available, adequate to screen and treat; and with transportation available for further diagnosis and treatment);

  Level II (there are a lot of victims and resources are not enough; help coming from various organisms at a regional level is needed- the definition varies according to the size and kind of territorial organisation of the country);

  Level III (the harm is massive; local and regional resources available are insufficient and the deficiencies are so significant national or international help is needed.

- **Social Vulnerability:** Social vulnerability refers to the inability of people, organizations, and societies to withstand adverse impacts from multiple stressors to which they are exposed. These impacts are due in part to characteristics inherent in social interactions, institutions, and systems of cultural values.

Vulnerability decreases with the degree of development of civilisation, which in essence precisely aims to protect human beings from the negative consequences of their behaviour and from the forces unleashed by nature (Gilbert, 1958).

- **Scapegoating in Disasters:** Disasters are a great opportunity to appoint scapegoats; efforts to lay the burden of guilt on a person or groups are constant. According to Allinson (1993), "Whenever a single cause for any event is sought in the human realm, it is thus very natural for one to look for who, as a singular agent, is responsible. If the event in question is a disaster, then the first inclination is to look for whose fault it is. Once blame can be assigned, the existence of the disaster will have been explained. Finding the guilty party or parties solves the disaster 'problem'. Of course it does not. What it does do, however, is to create the appearance of a solution, and this appearance of a solution cannot assist".
- **A Disaster Unmasks False Myths:** A disaster is an empirical falsification of human action, the proof of the incorrectness of human being's conceptions on nature and culture. Not only structures and social functioning are affected; many mental schemes also break down.
- **Hazards, Disasters and Catastrophe:** A hazard, or natural hazard, is any natural process that poses a threat to human life or property. The event itself is not a hazard; rather, a process becomes a hazard when it threatens human interests.

  A disaster, or natural disaster, is the effect of a hazard on society, usually as an event that occurs over a limited time span in a defined geographic area. The term disaster is used when the interaction between humans and a natural process results in significant property damage, injuries, or loss of life.

  A catastrophe is a massive disaster requiring significant expenditure of time and money of recovery.

Q5. Discuss the various causes and impacts of draught.

Ans. Causes of draught: Three drought types discussed above are completely different from one another. There are several causes due to which drought can occur. Some of the main causes are:

- Monsoon variations - failure or erratic behaviour of monsoon can cause considerable amount of pressure; such situations may create drought like situations.
- Overexploitation of surface and ground water - inadequate water conservation measures may result in situations where water availability reduced considerably during summers, which may lead to drought like situations.
- Changing agricultural practices may also lead to drought like situations. When cropping patterns change from low to moderate water demand crops to high demand crops, water consumption increases to grow the crops exerting pressure on existing meager irrigation facilities and other available resources of water supply.
- Over exploitation and mismanagement or poor management of water resources for residential and irrigational purpose may lead to such situations.

Drought Impacts: When drought begins, the agricultural sector is usually the first to be affected because of its heavy dependence on stored soil water (also on surface and sub-surface water supplies), which can be rapidly depleted during extended dry periods. Usually, during drought, soil water reserves are replenished first, followed by stream-flow, reservoirs and lakes, and ground water. If precipitation deficiencies continue, then people dependent on other sources of water will begin to feel the effects of the shortage. Those who rely on surface water (i.e., reservoirs and lakes) and subsurface water (i.e., ground water), for example, are usually the last to be affected.

In the after drought period, ground water users, often the last to be affected by drought during its onset, may be last to experience a return to normal water levels. The length of the recovery period is a function of the intensity of the drought, its duration, and the quantity of precipitation received as the episode terminates.

The impacts of drought can be generally divided into three major groups: Economic Impacts, Environmental Impacts and Social Impacts.

Economic Impacts: General economic impacts include:

- Decreased land prices.

- Loss to industries directly dependent on agricultural production (e.g., machinery and fertilizer manufacturers, food processors, dairies, etc.).
- Unemployment from drought-related declines in production.
- Strain on financial institutions (foreclosures, more credit risk, capital shortfalls).
- Revenue losses to federal, state, and local governments (from reduced tax base).
- Reduction of economic development.
- Fewer agricultural producers (due to bankruptcies, new occupations).
- Rural population loss.

Environmental Impacts: Environmental losses are the result of damages to plant and animal species, wildlife habitat, and air, soil and water quality. Some of the effects are short-term and conditions quickly return to normal following the end of drought. Other effects linger for some time or may even become permanent. They are mainly caused by:

- Increased number and severity of fires - forest fires destroying thousands of acres of lands, urban and rural fires exacerbated by the lack of water to distinguish the fires, etc.
- Haze caused by fires, affecting air quality and reduced visibility - due to excessive presence of dusts and pollutants, exacerbated by reduced fire fighting capability (lack of water) Wind erosion of soils
- Desertification
- Reduction and degradation of fish and wildlife habitat due to lack of feed and drinking water, disease and increased vulnerability to predation (species concentrated near water)
- Migration and concentration of wild animals - loss of wildlife in some areas and too many wildlife in other areas
- Damage to plant species due to lack of water and plant diseases.

In additional, severe hydrological effects can be detected in lowered water levels in reservoirs, lakes and ponds and reduced stream-flow and springs. Loss of wetlands in turn leads to loss of biodiversity and fish habitats. Drying up of estuaries trigger changes in salinity levels. The increased groundwater depletion produce land subsidence and ultimately impact on the quality of water (e.g., salt concentration, increased water temperature, rising PH level, turbidity).

Social Impacts: Social impacts mainly involve public safety, health, conflict between water users, reduced quality of life and inequities in the distribution of impacts and disaster relief. Many of the impacts specified as economic and environmental have social components as well. In general, social impacts can be further subdivided into four major areas as shown in the table below:

Key areas	Impacts
Health	• Mental and physical stress (anxiety, depression, loss of security, domestic violence) • Health-related low-flow problems (cross-connection contamination of drinking water sources, diminished sewage flows, increased pollutant concentrations, decreased quality of water, etc.) • Reductions in nutrition (high-cost food limitations, stress-related dietary deficiencies) • Loss of human life (heat stroke, malnutrition) • Loss of animals' lives (malnutrition, shortage of fodder, outbreak of disease caused by wildlife concentrations, other infections like worms) • Public safety from forest and range fires (increased respiratory ailments from smokes and haze, increased pollutants in the air) • Famine (food shortage caused by low production yield, spread of disease to animals and plants, locust invasion)
Conflicts	• Water user conflicts (upstream vs. downstream, rich vs. poor, rural vs. urban) • Political conflicts (e.g., inequality in drought response, inefficiency in handling drought management, withholding of information) • Management conflicts (mainly related to political conflicts) • Other social conflicts (e.g., scientific, media-based)
Quality of life/changes in lifestyle	• Disruption of cultural belief systems (e.g., religious and scientific views of natural hazards) • Loss of cultural sites and other important landmarks

	(loss of aesthetic values) • Increased poverty in general (e.g., mounting debts for the poor, increased credit risks, increased rural unemployment) • Mass migrations (rural to urban areas, cross-border migrations) • Reduction or modification of recreational activities (decreased incomes, lesser choice of recreational activities)
Drought response	• Perceptions of inequity in relief distribution, possibly related to socioeconomic status, ethnicity, age, gender, seniority • Lack of data/information • Lack of coordination and dissemination • Loss of confidence in government

Q6. Write short notes on the followings:

(i) Stampede

Ans. A stampede is uncontrolled concerted running as an act of mass impulse among herd animals or a crowd of people in which the group collectively begins running, often in an attempt to escape a perceived threat. Non-human species associated with stampede behavior include zebras, cattles, elephants, blue wildebeests, walruses, wild horses, and rhinoceroses.

Types of Stampede: Incidents of stampedes can occur in numerous socio-situations. The causes and gravity of these situations vary from each other. The following list provides a fair idea about various types of situations where stampedes can occur:

- Air raid shelter
- Entertainment events
- Escalator and moving walkways
- Food distribution
- Funeral procession
- Natural disasters
- Power failure
- Religious events
- Fire incidents in religious/other events
- Riots

- Sports events
- Weather related

Causes: Causes of stampedes can be better understood through the FIST MODEL, which describes the primary elements involved in crowd disasters. In other words, the elements provide a model for understanding the causes of crowd disasters, means of prevention, and possible mitigation of an ongoing crowd incident. The acronym "FIST" is defined as follows: FORCE (F) of the crowd, or crowd pressure; INFORMATION (I) upon which the crowd acts or reacts, real or perceived, true or false: SPACE (S) involved in the crowd incident, standing area, physical facilities stairs, corridors, escalators; TIME (T) duration of incident, event scheduling, facility processing rates.

Dos' and Don'ts

- One must be very alert to the fact that some pilgrims of certain nationalities come in bunches and batches and push their way through. Pilgrims should not get into their way or try to stop them as one could get harmed in the process. It will be more sensible to avoid their path and wait till they get out.
- It is advisable to move in groups from the camps with the assistance of the controlling authority or group leader or police person.
- Do not try to go against the direction of the crowd. Move with the crowd.
- Do not lose temper and do not fight with others. If requires, pilgrims can retrace steps after the rush has passed.
- Understand the evacuation routes, emergency exits and layout of the place of event.
- Keep calm. Don't panic.
- In case of emergency do not run.
- Think before you do. Do not just blindly follow others.
- Open area is safer. On exit try to get away in diverse directions.
- Follow instructions given by the authorities, public address system etc.
- Do not spread rumors.

- Assist and collaborate with the organizers, authorities, fire services Police etc.
- Try to help others in your best capable way.

(ii) Forest fires

Ans. The most common hazard in forests is forests fire. Forests fires are as old as the forests themselves. They pose a threat not only to the forest wealth but also to the entire regime to fauna and flora seriously disturbing the bio-diversity and the ecology and environment of a region. During summer, when there is no rain for months, the forests become littered with dry senescent leaves and twinges, which could burst into flames ignited by the slightest spark. The Himalayan forests, particularly, Garhwal Himalayas have been burning regularly during the last few summers, with colossal loss of vegetation cover of that region.

Causes of Forest Fire: Human beings are the number one cause of wildfires in the United States. Many of these wildfires are caused by cigarette butts being left on the land, campfires that have been left unmonitored, as well as intentional acts of arson. 90% of the wildfires in the U.S. are caused by people. Below are few of the man-made causes of wildfires.

(1) Burning Debris: It is pretty common to burn yard waste in many places. While it is legal to do so, it may cause fires at many places when things go out of hand. Winds play a major role in wildfires. They can cause flames of a burning debris to spread into forests or farms or fields.

(2) Unattended Campfires: Camping can be of great fun for both young and old age people. Unattended campfires can put things out of control and can cause wildfires. It is therefore recommended to choose safe location for a campfire that is away from ignitable objects and is stocked with a bucket of water and a shovel.

(3) Equipment Failure or Engine Sparks: A running engine can spew hot sparks when things go wrong. Car crashes have been known to start fires quickly and that is why it is common to see firefighters rush to the scene in anticipation of a fire. Small engine sparks can give way to high flames if that vehicle is operating in a field or a forest.

(4) Cigarettes: Cigarettes are another common cause of wildfires. It is common for people to throw the cigarette bud on the ground knowing that it is still burning. Smokers must understand that a small negligence on their part can cause huge impact on the environment and surrounding areas.

(5) Fireworks: Fireworks are fun to shoot off but special care needs to be taken when they are in the hands of amateurs. Fireworks must be avoided even when there is small chance that they could start a wildfire. If not handled properly that may end up as flames in unwanted **territory.**

(6) Arson: Arson is the act of setting fire to property, vehicles or any other thing with the intention to cause damage. A person who commits this crime is called an arsonist. Arson is sometime done by people to their own property in order to receive compensation. Arson may account for 30% of all wildfire cases.

Mother Nature is responsible for other 10% of wildfires in the United States.

(1) Lightening: Lightening can cause wildfires, especially the type of lightning called "hot lightning", which can last for a relatively long time. When it strikes, it can produce a spark which can set off a forest or a field.

(2) Volcanic Eruption: Hot burning lava, from volcanic eruptions, also causes wildfires.

Types of Forest Fire: Forest fires differ depending upon its nature, size, spreading speed, behavior etc. basically this can be sub-grouped into four types depending upon their nature and size as follows:

(1) Underground Fire: Underground fire is the fire of low intensity consuming the organic matter beneath and the surface litter of forest floor is sub-grouped as underground fire. In most of the dense forests occurring in the wetter parts of Himalayas, a thick mantle of organic matter is found on top of the mineral soil. This fire spreads in by consuming such materials. These fires usually spread entirely underground and burn for some meters below the surface and spreads very slowly and in most cases it becomes very hard to detect and control such type of fires. They may continue to burn for months and destroy vegetative cover of the soil.

(2) Surface Fires: Surface fire is the most common forest fires that burn undergrowth and dead material along the floor of the forest. In general it is very useful for the forest growth and regeneration. If grow in size this fire not only burns ground flora but also results to engulf the undergrowth and the middle story of the forest. Surface fires spread by flaming combustion through fuels at or near the surface grass dead and down limbs, forest needle and leaf litter, or debris from harvesting or land clearing. Thus as surface fire is "A fire that burns surface litter, other loose debris of the forest floor and small vegetation. This is the most common type of fire in timber stand of all species. It may be a mild, low-energy fire in sparse grass and pine needle litter, or it may be a very hot, fast moving fire where slash, flammable under story shrubs or other abundant fuel prevails. A surface fire if spreads, may burn up to the taller vegetation and tree crowns as it progresses.

(3) Ground Fires: There is no clear distinction between underground and ground fires. The smoldering for sometime under ground fires changes into Ground fire. This fire burns root and other material on or beneath the surface i.e. burns the herbaceous growth on forest floor together with the layer of organic matter in various stages of decay. They are more damaging than surface fires and they can destroy vegetation completely. These fires are fires in the sub-surface organic fuels, such as duff layers under forest stands, Arctic tundra or taiga, and organic soils of swamps or bogs. Ground fires burn underneath the surface by smoldering combustion and are most often ignited by surface fires. Thus a Ground Fire consumes the organic material beneath the surface litter of the forest floor and fighting such fires is very difficult and tedious job.

(4) Crown Fires: Crown fire is the most unpredictable fire, which burns the top of trees and spread rapidly by wind. In most of the cases surface fires invariably ignite these fires. Thus a Crown Fire is a fire that advances from top to top of trees or shrubs more or less Independently of the surface fire. In dense conifer stands on steep slopes or on level ground, with a brisk wind, the crown fire may race ahead of the supporting surface fire. This is most spectacular kind of forest fire. Since it is over the heads of ground force it is uncontrollable until it again drops to the ground, and since it is usually fast moving it poses grave danger to the fire fighters becoming trapped and burned.

(5) Firestorms: Among the forest fire, the fires spreading most rapidly are the firestorm, which is an intense fire over a large area. As the fire burns, heat rises and airs rushes in, causing the fire to grow. More air makes the fire spin violently like a storm. Flames fly out from the base and burning ember spew out the top of the fiery twister, starting smaller fires around it. Temperatures inside these storms can reach around 2,000 degrees Fahrenheit.

Do's and Don'ts: Creating awareness among citizens can play very significant role in prevention and control of forest fires. Advertisement through local media like radio, television, pamphlets, signboards, papers, panchayats etc. may be very effective in this regard. Teaching people about the do's and don'ts to prevent and control forest fire may be effective tool of forest fire management techniques.

What to do before and during forest fire?

Do's

- Take appropriate preventive measures before fire season, i.e., cutting fire line, removal of dry litters from the forest, etc.
- Make people aware about the causes and adverse impacts of forest fire.
- Do apply seasonal mitigation measures before fire season, i.e., reduction of fuel, removal of dry timber from forest etc.
- If there is a fire, try to put the fire out by digging or circle around it by water or by bushes, if not possible inform fire brigade or forest officials.
- In case of fire, move farm animals and movable property to safer places.
- Follow the effective monitoring and warning system.
- Encourage people to leave the tradition of shifting cultivation and collection of Minor Forest Produces by burning fire in the forest area.

Don'ts

- One should not throw smoldering cigarette butt or bidi in or near the forest.
- The burning wood should not be left by picnicker or other people working in the forest.
- Don't enter the forest during the fire.
- Don't lift the dry litter during summer season
- Don't be scared, be calm and encourage others to suppress the fire.

(iii) Air Accidents

Ans. Air accidents are by and large of three types; mid-air collisions, forced landings, crash due to technical snags and air-crash in mountainous terrain due to poor visibility. While air accidents can occur at any time and at any place, areas within about 30-40 kms radius of airports are most vulnerable. Past experience shows that majority of air accidents occur either during take-off or landing near about major airports where flight paths get congested. In addition, air accidents also take place at remote inaccessible places like forests, hilly and mountainous regions, high seas, etc. Causes of air accidents are either human failure of pilots, air traffic controllers or technical failures of on board, landing instruments. In rare cases it may also be the result of terrorist activities.

Causes of air accidents are either human failure of pilots, air traffic controllers or technical failures of on board landing instruments. In rare cases it may also be the result of terrorist activities.

(iv) Boat Accidents

Ans. With the increase in volume of inland boats and sea fishing, boat capsizing is a distinct possibility. The factors, which contribute to this disaster have been identified as partly due to natural hazards such as cyclones or floods and greater part has been the due to man-made causes such as over loading of the boat, poor quality of equipment in the boat, poor maintenance and consequent breakdown and of course human error of judgment. Boat accidents are found to occur mainly during the flood season, more so during bad weather and also under conditions of impaired visibility. Boats are more vulnerable during large gatherings such as melas, festivals etc. especially during their opening time when people want to reach early before its start or at closing time when there is a rush of people wanting to return home before night fall. Poor visibility at the time has also contributed to boat accidents especially those cases that take place due to collision. In many cases large number of boats gather during festivals, resulting in inadequate space for maneuvering the boat. Sometimes it may not be possible for authorities concerned to exercise full control on the river boat traffic due to non-availability of adequate security staff, logistic and other problems.

Boat accidents occur mainly due to overloading, overcrowding, unruly behavior, panic amongst passengers and capsizing. Overloading of the boat results in very low freeboard allowing water to enter the boat easily. Flash-floods and strong currents in the river also result in boat accidents, especially in cases where there are no proper communication available with boat operators regarding the weather. A major cause for boat accidents is lack of safety consciousness on the part of crew, which leads to unsafe situations such as overloading, overcrowing, sailing in adverse weather and collision.

(v) Oil Spills

Ans. Today the sea is being a key source of food, fresh water, and mineral including oil and natural gas and renewable energy. The rapid industrial growth in recent years and the tremendous increase in human population are generating huge quantities of waste materials to be disposed off from land. Thus, the use of marine environment as a dumping ground of waste material has been constantly on the increase and this has caused pollution of the marine environment. In addition to industrialization and increase in population, urbanization, deforestation, increase in number and size of ships, demand for oil, oily wastes arising from ships, tankers and offshore installation, chemicals and dangerous goods, dumping of nuclear waste and leakage of under water pipelines is a long list being one of the causes of marine pollution in our coastal waters. Areas having off shore oil installations, under sea pipelines, sea routes traversed by oil tankers, refineries and under ground pipelines for oils transportation are vulnerable to oil spills.

Causes of oil spills are invariably leakage somewhere in the pipeline. Leakage in the pipeline in turn can be due to a variety of reasons such as sub-standard pipes, corrosion of metal, pipes having outlived their life, poor maintenance etc. Factors that contribute to oil spills are:

(1) Collision at sea: Due to transit of number of tankers in the area to transport oil from oil extraction platforms, the eventuality of tanker collision off the coast resulting in spill and turning into major oil spill catastrophe cannot be ruled out,

(2) oil extraction activities: Defect/malfunctioning of oil extension pipe line/oil spill in the vicinity of oil extraction platform is ever present. The changes of these oilrigs coming under the attack of our enemies during the hostility further enhances the chances of oil spill disaster scenario.

(3) Grounding: There have been number of instances where due to Navigational errors number of ships have run aground,

(4) Tanker routes pumping out of bilges: Due to various oil tankers transiting, accidental discharge on the oil route cannot be ruled out. Number of ships also find it convenient to pump out from bilges in Open Ocean and the bilges mostly contains the oil and

(5) Danger of spillage while transferring oil from ship to shore facilities: Danger of oil spillage always loom large when the oil is being transferred from the offshore terminal to the ship and from the ship to shore facilities in various ports

(vi) Rail Accidents

Ans. The Indian railways, is the largest railway system in Asia and the first largest railway system under a single management in the world. Railways is the principal mode of transport for both passengers and goods in the country. Railway is the life line of the nation particularly amongst the developing countries like India where infrastructure developments are accorded high priority to boost the nations wealth. The success of any transport organization is gauged by the parameters such as punctuality, reliability, safety, frequency and adaptability. In the course of the working, the railways are confronted with disasters arising out of cyclone, floods, fires, bomb blasts and accidents etc., involving trains. While a railway accident can occur at any stretch of railway track, experience has shown that portion of railway track having double line sections are particularly vulnerable to serious rail accidents.

Causes in most cases are human failure. Factors that contribute to Rail accidents are:

- Breaches of tanks due to heavy rains
- Cyclone/flash floods
- Human failures
- Equipment failures
- Heavy rains leading to washing away of the track/collapse of bridges
- Land slides
- Breach of rules on unmanned railway level crossing
- Sabotage
- Tampering with track
- Act of God

(vii) Road Accidents

Ans. Both National and state Highways are particularly vulnerable to serious road accidents since it is on these stretches that high speed accidents occurs. Apart from these, roads in hilly sections and ghat areas are also vulnerable to road accidents due to road vehicles falling into pits. The problem of road traffic accident has assumed alarming proposition with ever increasing number of motor vehicles competing for the limit paved space. The resultant congestion in traffic is inevitable and the consequences of congestion are road accidents. It is observed that loss of life and injuries in road accidents are high in developing countries as compared to the developed countries. It is interesting to note that while there is a reduction of deaths due to road accidents in the developed countries the picture emerging from the developing countries shows an abnormal increase. Road safety, as a problem, has been analyzed in many different ways.

Road accident is most unwanted thing to happen to a road user, though they happen quite often. The most unfortunate thing is that we don't learn from our mistakes on road. Most of the road users are quite well aware of the general rules and safety measures while using roads but it is only the laxity on part of road users, which cause accidents and crashes. Main cause of accidents and crashes are due to human errors. We are elaborating some of the common behaviour of humans which results in accident.

- **Over Speeding:** Most of the fatal accidents occur due to over speeding. It is a natural psyche of humans to excel. If given a chance man is sure to achieve infinity in speed. But when we are sharing the road with other users we will always remain behind some or other vehicle. Increase in speed multiplies the risk of accident and severity of injury during accident.
- **Drunken Driving:** Consumption of alcohol to celebrate any occasion is common. But when mixed with driving it turns celebration into a misfortune. Alcohol reduces concentration. It decreases reaction time of a human body. Limbs take more to react to the instructions of brain. It hampers vision due to dizziness. Alcohol dampens fear and incite humans to take risks. All these factors while driving cause accidents and many a times it proves fatal.

- **Distractions to Driver:** Though distraction while driving could be minor but it can cause major accidents.

  Distractions could be outside or inside the vehicle. The major distraction now a days is talking on mobile phone while driving. Act of talking on phone occupies major portion of brain and the smaller part handles the driving skills.
- **Red Light Jumping:** It is a common sight at road intersections that vehicles cross without caring for the light. The main motive behind Red light jumping is saving time. The common conception is that stopping at red signal is wastage of time and fuel. Studies have shown that traffic signals followed properly by all drivers saves time and commuters reach destination safely and timely. A red light jumper not only jeopardizes his life but also the safety of other road users.

(viii) Chemical disaster

Ans. The accidental release of large amounts of toxins into the environment. The effects suffered by people in the area are determined by the toxicity of the chemical, its speed in spreading, its composition (liquid, solid, or gaseous), and the spill site, esp. its proximity to a water supply or buildings. The major effect may be due to the chemical itself or to a resulting fire or explosion. The catastrophic release of chemicals may overwhelm, at least temporarily, local or regional health care resources.

Causes and Impacts:

Causes: A Chemical disaster may take place due to anyone or more ofthe following:

- An accident or explosion at the production facility of hazardous material.
- An accident at the storage facility of hazardous material.
- An accident during transportation of hazardous material through population centres.
- Inadequacies in toxic waste management. This results in long-term health effect on communities. Toxic waste can cause environmental pollution as well as ground water pollution.
- Failures in safety systems of chemical plants.

- Deliberate sabotage of a manufacturing area or storage facility of a hazardous chemical substance or a sabotage during transportation of such substance.
- Occurrence of natural disasters, such as, earthquakes, cyclones etc. can also trigger chemical disasters essentially through damage and destruction to chemical industrial units storing or producing hazardous material.

Impacts: Chemical disasters lead to serious and varied impacts. These can result into explosions and/or fires. The most hazardous impact of a chemical disaster lies in the extreme pollution of air, water and food chain upto life-threatening levels even. The long-term health impairment can even extend to coming generations.

A chemical disaster may result into one or all of the following:

- **Physical Damage:** This includes damage or destruction of structure and infrastructure. A transportation accident may damage the means of transport used for transporting hazardous material viz. vehicle, rail etc. Industrial fires, if not contained, may affect large areas.
- Casualties: Chemical disaster may result in large-scale casualties. While quick medical relief is essential to save lives, immediate disposal of dead bodies will also need planning.
- Environmental Damage: Chemical disasters affect the environment because of likely contamination of air, water supply, land, crops, vegetation and animal life. In some cases certain areas may become uninhabitable for humans and animals. The possibility of mega scale migration/evacuation/resettlement could loom large.

Sources of Chemical Disasters: The sources could be Manufacturing and Formulation Facility (including during Commissioning and Process Operation, Maintenance, Disposal and Waste Management), Material Handling and Storage, Bulk Storages in manufacturing facilities and isolated storages (including tank farms in Ports and Docks), Storages of Small Containers. In manufacturing facilities, in isolated warehouse and godowns, Storage of Fuels (LPG Depots etc.) and Pipelines, and Transportation (road, rail, air and waterways)

(ix) Terrorism

Ans. Terrorism is, in the broadest sense, the use of intentionally indiscriminate violence as a means to create terror among masses of people; or fear to achieve a financial, political, religious or ideological aim. It is used in this regard primarily to refer to violence against peacetime targets or in war against non-combatants. The terms "terrorist" and "terrorism" originated during the French Revolution of the late 18th century but gained mainstream popularity during the U.S. presidency of Ronald Reagan (1981–89) after the 1983 Beirut barracks bombings and again after the 2001 September 11 attacks and the 2002 Bali bombings.

Classification of Terrorism:

- **International Terrorism:** Acts of violence by national of one country against the citizens/state of another country.
- **State:** The state uses weapons of the state against its own people. Acts of violence and intimidation by the state against its own population e.g. Argentina's 'Dirty War'.
- **State-supported:** The state uses its weapons to attack other country acts of violence supported by an or funded by external state actors (Proxy war). Eg. RUF in Sierra Leone.
- **Sub-state:** A small group within the state is trying to use violence to accomplish its own goal.
- **Domestic:** Acts of violence by non-state actors against domestic political opponents. Domestic terrorism is of two types:
- Ideological (e.g. Marxist, Islamist)
- Ethnic e.g. ETA (Spain), GIA (Algeria)
- **Social revolutionary:** rebel against corrupt old ways (e.g. Baader- Meinhof gang in Germany)
- **National Separatists:** Trying to carry on the family mission (E.g. Palestinian Terrorists, Northern Irelanders).
- **Religious Fundamentalists:** they kill in the name of God. (E.g. Usama Bin Laden, abortion clinic bombers).
- **New Religion:** The cults defending new religions (e.g. Shinrikyo in Japan (sarin gas in subway).

- **Right Wing:** They see the government as they enemy and illegitimate. (E.g. Neo-Nazis, Timothy McVeigh, Klu Klux Klan).
- **Single Issue:** (e.g. animal rights, ecologic terrorism (usually single people willing to kill).

(x) Epidemics

Ans. An epidemic is the rapid spread of infectious disease to a large number of people in a given population within a short period of time, usually two weeks or less. For example, in meningococcal infections, an attack rate in excess of 15 cases per 100,000 people for two consecutive weeks is considered an epidemic.

Epidemics of infectious disease are generally caused by several factors including a change in the ecology of the host population (e.g. increased stress or increase in the density of a vector species), a genetic change in the pathogen reservoir or the introduction of an emerging pathogen to a host population (by movement of pathogen or host). Generally, an epidemic occurs when host immunity to either an established pathogen or newly emerging novel pathogen is suddenly reduced below that found in the endemic equilibrium and the transmission threshold is exceeded.

An epidemic may be restricted to one location; however, if it spreads to other countries or continents and affects a substantial number of people, it may be termed a pandemic. The declaration of an epidemic usually requires a good understanding of a baseline rate of incidence; epidemics for certain diseases, such as influenza, are defined as reaching some defined increase in incidence above this baseline. A few cases of a very rare disease may be classified as an epidemic, while many cases of a common disease (such as the common cold) would not.

Types of Epidemics: There are two major types of infectious diseases which can develop into epidemics: "common source" and "host-to-host". Common source epidemics arise from a contaminated source, such as water or food, while host-to-host infections are transmitted from one infected individual to another via various, perhaps indirect routes. Common source epidemics usually produce more new cases earlier and faster than host-to-host epidemics. Host-to-host epidemics. Host-to-host epidemics are slower to grow and slower to diminish. Anything causing disease is called a pathogen. A vector is an organism that serves as an intermediary in the transmission of a host-to-host disease. For instance, many infections are transmitted by mosquitoes, fleas, ticks, etc. to people. A fomite is any inanimate object that adheres to or transmits infectious material, e.g., bedding, clothing, surgical instruments, etc.

Impact: Epidemics and outbreaks of different communicable diseases have plagued mankind since time immemorial. According to estimates made by World Health Organisation, worldwide 17 million deaths were attributed to infectious diseases during 1997; hundreds of million were disabled and incapacitated with economic loss that defies any precise calculations. Advance in public health and medicine, sanitation and vector control have led to considerable prevention and control of these diseases in some countries, but have had minimal impact in the majority of developing countries of the world due to lack of funds. Moreover, within a country, there continues to be enormous disparities in mortality, disability and exposure to infection among social classes with the poor, socially backwards and children suffering extremes of ill-health in all societies.

Increased rates of morbidity and mortality due to communicable diseases occur more frequently in association with complex emergencies than other disasters. In many of these settings, especially those occurring in developing countries, between 60% and 90% of deaths have been attributed to one of four major infectious causes: measles, diarrhoea, acute respiratory infections and malaria. Acute malnutrition is often associated with increased case fatality rates of these diseases, especially among young children. There have also been outbreaks of other communicable diseases, such as meningococcal meningitis, yellow fever, viral hepatitis and typhoid, in certain settings.

Mitigation Measures: Significant improvements have taken place in health services in India during the past 58 years.

- **Current system of surveillance and mechanism to control the outbreak of endemic diseases:** For diseases with significant mortality and morbidity, the federal government has launched national Programmes which include malaria, tuberculosis, leprosy etc. Though the funding, technical designing as well as monitoring is done by the Central Government, the responsibility of implementation of these programmes rests with the respective state government.

- **National Programme for Surveillance of Communicable Disease (NPSCD):** Efforts have already been made by the Government of India to strengthen the health machinery for early detection of epidemic-prone diseases under its National Programme for surveillance of Communicable Diseases. The Government of India has launched National Surveillance Programme for Communicable Diseases (NSPCD) during 1997-98 as Central Scheme. The main objective of this programme is capacity building at the state and district levels for early identification of outbreaks of communicable diseases and appropriate and timely response to these outbreaks. The programme is being implemented by the state governments through their existing infrastructure. Under the programme, the surveillance system is strengthened through training of medical and paramedical personnel, dissemination of technical information and guidelines, up-gradation of laboratories, modernisation of communication and data processing system.

A strong public health and surveillance system is required for quick detection and control of communicable diseases. At present the public health infrastructure in India is inadequately prepared to sense early warning signals of outbreak of an epidemic and to respond in time.

(xi) Nuclear disaster

Ans. The occurrence of nuclear or radiological disaster is of the great concern. It is accompanied with sudden release of huge amount of harmful radiations or radioactive materials (Isotopes of Cesium, Cobalt, Iridium, Iodine, Srontium, Uranium, Plutonium etc.) or both together in environment in a small area. It is described as a disaster caused due to an extraordinary emission of radioactive material or radiation either through explosion of a nuclear bomb or in the operation of nuclear reactors and other nuclear related activities.

Causes

- **Intentional Use of Nuclear Weapons in the event of war:** With the advancement of scientific research, several countries have acquired the technology to produce Nuclear Arms, Which are more destructive and harmful than the atom bomb used more than half a century ago. Nuclear bombs have openly been used twice, both times by the United State against

Japan during World War II (1939-1945). On August 6, 1945, the city of Hiroshima was almost completely destroyed, and three days later the city of Nagasaki was bombed.

- **Accidental Explosion of Nuclear Weapons:** Nuclear weapons are designed with great care to explode only when deliberately armed and fired. Nevertheless, there is always a possibility that, as a result of accidental circumstances, an explosion will take place inadvertently and such accidents might occur in areas where weapons are assembled and stored, during the course of loading and transportation on the ground, or when actually in the delivery vehicle, e.g., an airplane or a missile.
- **Accidents in Nuclear Power Project:** There is also a risk of accidental exposure to harmful radiation from the several nuclear reactors used for generation of power. The potential threat from an accident at a nuclear power plant is exposure to radiation which would occur from the release of radioactive material into the environment and the area affected would depend on the amount of the release, wind direction and speed and weather conditions.
- **Terrorist Attacks or Dirty Bombs:** Through use of 'Radiological Dispersion Device' (ROD), an expedient weapon, wherein radioactive material is disseminated by using conventional explosives and debris is subsequently scattered across the targeted area. Also through other modes like attack of the nuclear power plant or facility using or processing radioactive material via air craft strike or bombardment with heavy munitions or sabotage.

Response: The emergency response actions will focus on reducing the effects of immediate effect that shall comprise-fire, destruction, damaged vegetation, dead, wounded human beings and animals, psychological phobia. This demands judicious planning, and multi-faceted preparations that shall include store management training, communication and command, etc surmount the nuclear emergency.

Do's and Don'ts

Do's:

- Plug ears, save skin from heat, put on head gear, know the explosion site and go away from ground zero, breath normally, stay calm.
- Lie down on ground with face down - head away from ground zero, cover face with handkerchief. It will avoid internal contamination
- If in shelter, close doors/windows, switch off AC and remain inside, evacuate, relocate, fallout may continue for more than 24 hours depending upon weather.
- Go underground to reduce external radiation and avoid external contamination.
- If contaminated, remove clothes and put them in poly bags, take showers, stay in tunnels, trenches, foxholes, tents vehicles decontaminate food or areas.
- Put on mask to avoid inhaling contaminated air.
- Put on protective suits, if available help injured. Become part of rescue team.
- Consume Bio-protectors like KI, KIO3, Beer, Tulsi, Arnica, Caffein, Diltiazem, Vitamin C/E, podophylum.
- Get treatment for burn, cut and other injuries.
- Keep monitoring radiation level/radiation dose

Don'ts:

- Do not look at blinding flash, don't go in to cloud/rain/fog.
- Do not run or get panicky
- Do not spread rumours.
- Do not crowd the site: Keep away
- Do not crowd hospitals/road/areas.
- Know the explosion site and do not go in downwind direction.
- Do not go the radioactive contaminated area.
- Do not remain in open air. Water is a good neutron shield.
- Do not spread radioactive contamination (External and Internal).

(xii) Biological disaster

Ans. Biological disaster refers to calamity caused by the exposure of living organisms to germs and toxic substances. For instance, spread of a disease, a virus, an epidemic, and a locust plague. It belongs to the class of natural disasters.

Causes and impacts:

- **Natural outbreaks:** Natural outbreaks of disease may become epidemics and assume disastrous proportion if not contained in the initial stages.
- **Use of Biological Agents by Terrorists:** Use of biological agents to cause death, disability of damage mainly to human beings to prevail mass panic and slow mass casualties and an intentional use of biological agents to cause disease or death through dissemination of micro-organism or toxins in food or water or insect vector or by aerosol to harm human population, food crops and livestock.

Mode of Delivery: Biological agents can be dispersed by spraying them into the air, by infecting animals that carry the disease to human, and by contaminating food and water.

- **Aerosols:** biological agents are dispersed into the air, forming a fine mist that may drift for miles. Inhaling the agent may cause epidemic diseases in human beings or animals.
- **Animals:** Some diseases are spread by insects and animals, such as fleas, mice, flies, mosquitoes, and livestock.
- **Food and water contamination:** Some pathogenic organisms and toxins may persist in food and water supplies. Most microbes can be killed, and toxins deactivated, by cooking food and boiling water. Most microbes are killed by boiling water for one minute, but some require longer.
- **Person-to-person:** spread of a few infectious agents is also possible. Humans have been the source of infection for smallpox, plague, and the Lassa viruses.

Impact: Even a small-scale biological attack with a weapon grade agent on an urban center could cause massive morbidity and mortality, rapidly overwhelming the local medical capabilities. For example, an aerosolized release of little as 100kg of anthrax spores upwind of a metro city of a size of Washington DC has been estimated to have the potential to cause up to three millions of deaths.

Do's and don'ts: A biological attack is the release of germs or other biological substances. The germs must be inhaled, enter through a cut in the skin or be eaten to make you sick. Some biological agents can cause contagious diseases, others do not. Further, a biological attack may or may not be immediately obvious. One may probably learn of the danger through an emergency radio or TV broadcast. In rural areas, a loudspeaker or other methods such as used for a cyclone warning may be used to warn you.

Before: Children and older adults are particularly vulnerable to biological agents. Ensure from a doctor/the nearest hospital that all the required or suggested immunization are up to date.

During: In the event of a biological attack, public health officials may not immediately be able to provide information on what you should do. It will take time to determine what the illness is, how it should be treated, and who is in danger. Watch television, listen to radio, or check the interest for official news and information including signs and symptoms of the disease, areas in danger, if medications or vaccinations are being distributed, and where you should seek medical attention if you become ill.

After: Pay close attention to all official warnings and instructions on how to proceed. The delivery of medical services for a biological event may be handled differently to respond to increased demand. The basic public health procedures and medical protocols for handling exposure to biological agents are the same as for any infectious disease.

Q7. Describe the response action needed during accident.

Ans. Accident victims succumb to injuries due to shock, bleeding and head injuries. If necessary first aid and replacement of fluid can be arranged within the first hour of injury many lives could be saved. "The first hour is called the golden hour". Common injuries include crush injuries, fractures, bleeding and victims in a state of shock. In case of all accidents involving casualties and injuries:

- Inform the nearest traffic police station, post through passing vehicles on either side.
- Look for and rescue the injured or those still trapped inside.
- Arrange for transport of the injured to the nearest medical care center by first available means.
- Place dead bodies on one side to avoid obstructions.

- Traffic control should be organised locally using available manpower to avoid traffic jams.
- Discourage people from crowding near the accident spot
- Prevent people from looting goods from the accident site.

Air Accidents: In cases where the accident occurs beyond visual contact of the Aerodrome Control Tower, information of such accident is preceded by information of aircraft missing or contact having been lost with the Air Traffic Control. In case of a mid-air collision or an air crash into mountainous terrain, not much rescue work is possible since most passengers on board would have perished instantaneously. In case of forced landing, some amount of rescue work would still be possible by means of evacuating passengers from the crippled air-craft and moving them to safety.

Boat Accidents: Rescue boat passengers, give first aid and rush to nearby hospitals. In situations, where it is not possible to provide rescue, relief operations at short notice, it becomes necessary that administrative authorities concerned should periodically review logistics and other arrangements that may be required for such operations. In cases, where the number of crew members on the boat and life saving equipments like life jackets, inflatable rafts etc. are inadequate, it forces the passengers to either swim or else wait for some form of rescue team to arrive from close by locations so, under these conditions, the only response possible has to be provided by local people living nearby in immediate vicinity of the waterway.

Oil Spills: Once an oil spill is reported, members of response and base team shall be notified and base control room should be established and contact number of base control room should be reported to all concerned for effective co-ordination. On-scene coordinator who should be a senior level executive trained in oil spill management must immediately take charge of base control room after reporting of spill.

Rail Accidents: The guard and driver of the train should inform the local divisional control office regarding occurrence of the above accident. Divisional office in turn must organize rescue and relief work by way of ordering Accident Relief Medical Van and Accident Relief Train to be rushed to the site of accident. Normally, it takes railway's medical and rescue teams 3 to 4 hours time to arrive at the accident site. During this initial period, it is the local population that helps organize rescue and relief work along with railway staff traveling one the accident affected train.

Road Accidents: In such cases involving passenger carrying vehicles: Inform the nearest traffic police station and fire brigade; Look for and rescue the injured or those trapped in vehicles; Arrange for transport of the injured to the nearest medical center, Place dead bodies on one side to avoid obstructions; Traffic control should be organized locally using available manpower to avoid traffic jams; Discourage people from crowding near the accident spot, In case such accidents involve hazardous chemical, do not go anywhere near the accident spot since contents may explode or catch fire and prevent people at the accident site from lighting matches for cigarettes etc.

Q8. Elaborate the following disaster related incidents:

(i) Bhopal gas leak

Ans: The accident occurred on the night of 2-3 December 1984 at the Union Carbide Factory at Bhopal producing pesticides.

About 40 tonnes of Methyl Iso-Cynate (MIC) and other toxic gases including Hydrogen Cyanide (HCM) leaked from the plant. The gas affected the residents of Bhopal in a big way. Most affected were those staying in the localities downwind in the vicinity of the plant. About 8000 persons were killed. Health of more than 530,000 persons were severely affected causing multi-system injuries.

Thirty-six municipal wards were affected. The toxic gas was absorbed into the blood stream of the people causing lasting and damaging effect to lungs, brain, kidney, reproductive, as well as immune.

Causes of Disaster: The Bhopal Gas Disaster was caused by a complex set of independent human, organisational and technological errors. The salient aspects are summarized below:

Human Factors

- Inadequate safety training of employees.
- Low employee morale.
- Lack of awareness regarding the hazard potential of the plant among the managers and workers.
- Overlooking minor indicators of a possible accident occurred on earlier occasions. (There was a technical snag in storage

tank E-610 on 21 October 1984 which was ignored and not investigated)

Organisational Factors

- Lack of resources and inadequate managerial attention, which contributed to lower safety standards
- Lack of urgency in preparing contingency plans for possible accidents in the plant.

Technological Factors

- Numerous design errors
- Absence of computerised early warning system.
- Long-term storage of huge quantities of MIC.
- Outmoded manual safety system. (An electronically controlled four stages back-up safety system was used in similar plants elsewhere).
- Poor maintenance.

Certain Observations on Response to the Disaster: The medical facilities were over stretched. Besides, the doctors in Bhopal were not aware of the possible cause of the disaster. They were unaware of the type of gas, which had leaked out, and its toxicity. The plant officials insisted that MIC was not lethal; it was only an irritant.

There was no awareness of the hazard potential of the plant among politicians, government officials, media and the general population. This resulted in a total lack of preparedness to meet the eventuality of a disaster of such a magnitude. There was no credible public information system in place that resulted in total confusion, fear and panic.

Lesson Learnt from the Disaster: Environmental impact assessment of hazardous units is an inescapable necessity. Public education and awareness towards hazards of toxic material are important. Need for developing high standards of operator skills and safety in industrial units. Lack of contingency plan to meet possible emergency situation. It is important to work on, and be prepared for worst-case scenario.

Mandatory safety audits should be implemented that will ensure safety.

A comprehensive medical emergency plan should be prepared. In addition, the medical fraternity should also be trained and be prepared to handle mass casualties with prior knowledge of the toxic chemicals causing the disasters and with adequate medicines and supporting systems.

(ii) Surat plague

Ans. The 1994 plague in India was an outbreak of bubonic and pneumonic plague in south-central and western India from 26 August to 18 October 1994. 693 suspected cases and 56 deaths were reported from the five affected Indian states as well as the Union Territory of Delhi. These cases were from Maharashtra (488 cases), Gujarat (77 cases), Karnataka (46 cases), Uttar Pradesh (10 cases), Madhya Pradesh (4 cases) and New Delhi (68 cases). There are no reports of cases being exported to other countries.Some of the major observations, which could be noted as lessons for improving biological disaster response, are listed below:

Conditions before the outbreak of Plague

- Congestion in town.
- Inadequate garbage disposal arrangements.
- Lack of functional disease surveillance organisations.
- Lack of overall preparedness on behalf of civic administration to combat outbreak of an epidemic of this nature.

Conditions during the outbreak of Plague

- Paucity of drugs.
- Rumour mongering - there was a rumour that water in the city was poisoned.
- Lack of credible public information system.
- Lack of co-ordination within the medical authorities as well as in various government departments,
- No plans existed for moving people to safer areas.
- No public health programme to educate common masses to cope with plague epidemic was m vogue,
- Lack of judicial provisions to enforce medical practitioners to fulfill their social obligations. A number of private medical practitioners fled the town and many private nursing homes closed down.
- Inadequacy of medical infrastructure to handle a disaster of such a dimension. It was very creditable on part of medical personnel to work under great odds. At places even the medical personnel did not have protective gowns and the

sanitary staff ofthe municipal corporation worked without masks and gloves.

(iii) Uphaar Cinema fire

Ans. The Uphaar Cinema fire was one of the worst fire tragedies in the country. A total of 59 people lost their lives in the fire that broke out during the screening of Hindi film Border. The source of fire was a transformer in basement where a three phase terminal box of the transformer became loose due to overheating. The casualties were 57 dead (24 men, 20 women, 13 children) and 105 injured (62 men, 31 women, 12 children). There were 19 cars, eight scooters and 11 bicycles damaged. The chronology of events was as under.

12 June 1997	:	Technical stag and fire in transformer, fire extinguished but transformer not repaired and the shows continued.
13 June 1997	:	Short-circuit.
4.45 PM		- Transformer bursts, boiling oil spills out, power cut twice during the show, management thought it is another power cut, generator is put on. - Oil catches fire and petrol tanks in vehicles parked underground blow up, fire spreads rapidly through the parking lot. - Airconditioners ducts circulate smoke even faster throughout the halls and smoke gets thicker and denser. - Rear stalls vacated hastily, doors finally broken under pressure. - Heat so strong basement roof melted smashing parked cars.
5.20 PM	:	Fire brigades arrive
6.40 PM	:	Fire is brought under control.

The main disadvantage of this cinema theatre observed were:

- Situated at a very densely populated place.
- No clear passage for movement.
- Underground parking.

- Exits not clear.
- Complete blackout.
- Busy traffic.
- Limited space for parking and deployment of fire brigade and police vans.
- Unsafe electrical equipment.
- No fire fighting equipment and no trained personnel.
- Inflammable material.
- Illegal connections.
- No Fire extinguishers in working condition.

(iv) The chernobyl accident

Ans. Chemoby1 is located in Ukraine, erstwhile USSR. On 26th April 1986 one of the atomic reactors in the Chernoby1 Nuclear Power Plant had a core melt down. It is believed that the accident occurred due to human error as at the time of accident the plant was partly shutdown and certain safety mechanisms had been relaxed or disabled. This accident resulted in a fire at the power plant and a huge quantity of radioactive isotopes leaked out in the atmosphere and spread in the nearby areas.

Impact

(1) About 134 persons suffered from acute radiation sickness immediately. 28 of them died.

(2) About 135,000 personnel were evacuated from the areas in the proximity of the disaster site.

(3) The radioactive release is said to have affected 17 million people to varying degrees.

(4) About 155,000 square kilometers of area containing a population of 7 million was affected.

(5) About 800,000 personnel were pressed into service by the Soviet government for decontamination. Upto 45 percent of these persons also received unacceptable doses of radioactivity.

(6) Though the disaster occurred due to human error, the design of the plant was also an important factor.

Q9. Discuss the evolution of disaster management system in India.

Ans. Disaster management in India has evolved from an activity-based reactive setup to a proactive institutionalized structure; from single faculty domain to a multi-stakeholder setup; and from a relief-based approach to a 'multi-dimensional pro-active holistic approach for reducing risk'. The beginnings of an institutional structure for disaster management can be traced to the British period following the series of disasters such as famines of 1900, 1905, 1907 & 1943, and the Bihar-Nepal earthquake of 1937. Over the past century, the disaster management in India has undergone substantive changes in its composition, nature and policy

India and its people have coped with disasters since time immemorial. The present disaster management system in India has its roots in drought response and famine management in the late eighteenth century. The Commission issued its report in 1880, determining the principles and practices to be followed in future famines. A Famine Insurance Fund was developed, which set aside £1000, 000 a year for famine relief. In 1883, the first modern codification of famine response was framed, which classified situations of food scarcity according to a scale of intensity, and it laid out a series of steps that governments were obligated to take in the event of a famine. The code continues to influence contemporary policies through the well-entrenched relief management mechanism of India.

Institutional Structure 1947- June 2002: After Independence, in 1947, the initial focus was on food scarcity and famine; so the Scarcity Relief Division within the Ministry of Agriculture was delegated the nodal charge of drought and scarcity management. Armed with the experience of managing drought hazards, the Scarcity Relief Division was gradually given the responsibility of managing all natural disasters and upgraded to Natural Disaster Management Division (NDM Division) within the Ministry of Agriculture. However, it was felt that each disaster created complex emergencies that call for a broader and more holistic approach for effective management.

In the federal structure of the India administration, disaster management has been the responsibility of the states; with the national government performing a supportive role. The basic responsibility for undertaking rescue, relief and rehabilitation measures in the event of natural disasters is that of the concerned State Governments, particularly the district administration. The supportive role of the Central

Government refers to assistance in warning, transport, inter-state movement of food grains, financial assistance etc.

Institutional Structure after 2002: The frequent disasters and relief-centric approach ensured that India developed a well-structured response system after Independence. At the national level, the Ministry of Home Affairs is entrusted with the nodal responsibility of managing disasters. However, in view of the highly technical and specific nature of response of technological disaster events like aviation disasters, rail accidents, chemical disasters etc, ministries dealing with the particular subject have the nodal responsibility of handling that particular disaster.

The policy and institutions system for managing disasters has been well established over time. The Ministry of Home Affairs coordinates all matters concerning disaster management at the national level through the following officials/institutions:

Nodal Office in MHA: Within the Ministry of Home Affairs, the Central Relief Commissioner (CRC) is the nodal officer to coordinate relief operations for natural disasters. The CRC receives information on Early Warning and forecasting from the India Meteorological Department (IMD) and Central Water Commission (CWC) on a continuing basic.

Crisis Management Group: Along with the nodal ministry, the Crisis Management Group (CMG), under the Home Secretary coordinates management of any crisis situation including calamities in the country. The group constitutes all ministries/departments/organisations concerned with primary and secondary functions relating to the management of disasters. A nodal officer, nominated from each ministry/department is responsible for preparing the sectoral action plain/Emergency Support Function Plan for managing disasters. The CMG's functions are to review the Contingency plans, identify measures required for dealing with natural disasters, coordinate the activities of the Central Ministries and State governments in relation to disaster management and relief. In the event of a disaster, the CMG meets frequently to review the relief operations and extend all possible assistance required by the affected states to overcome the situation effectively. However after the passage of the Disaster Management Act 2005 the CMG has been subsumed into the National Executive Committee under the Home Secretary with all line ministries as members with a mandate of planning and implementation of all guidelines, thus widening the mandate to mitigation and prevention in addition to earlier responsibilities of preparedness and response.

At a higher level, the National Crisis Management Committee (NCMC) is headed by the Cabinet Secretary, who is the highest executive officer. Secretaries of all concerned ministries/departments are members of NCMC, which gives directions to the CMG as deemed necessary. The NCMC can give directions to any ministry/department/organization for specific action needed for meeting the crisis situation.

Major issues relating to natural disasters as placed before the Cabinet Committee on Natural Calamities. In case of calamities which impinge on internal security or which may be caused due to use of nuclear, biological and chemical weapons/materials, the matter is required to be placed before the Cabinet Committee on Security.

Q10. Describe the paradigm shift in disaster management system.

Ans. Definition –The shift in thinking and focus from a relief-centric approach to a more proactive, holistic and integrated approach for management of disasters through improved disaster

- Preparedness,
- Prevention,
- Mitigation, and
- Emergency response

is broadly considered as the paradigm shift.

Paradigm shift is the change in the way of thinking. The transformation in thinking is fuelled by agents of change and occurs through a process of evolution. Historically disaster management has been a reactive process. As disaster research evolved, it was observed that it is often not possible to stop hazardous occurrences, but preventive measures can be taken to minimize the adverse impacts of the hazards. The term 'Disaster Risk Reduction' is used to mention such measures. The paradigm shift in fact focuses on implementing these risk reduction measures. It is a shift in approach from:

- reactive approach where actions are taken after the disasters occur, e.g. providing

- humanitarian assistance, relief etc. to proactive approach where holistic integrated planning and management of disaster is;
- envisioned, e.g. building seismically protected structures, creating legislations, frameworks and guidelines for disaster management, setting up of emergency operating centers and response forces, generating a culture of prevention capacity building etc.

In other words, it aims at addressing the root causes of prospective disasters rather than addressing the stress and shocks arising after disasters.

For example, Indonesia is seismically active and prone to earthquakes. Between 2010 and 2016, Indonesia has experienced 11 earthquakes varying in magnitudes from 6.1 to 8.6. To minimize the risk of life losses and injuries, the earthquake preparedness program in schools in Bengkulu, Indonesia was carried out. Based on technical guidance cost effective retrofitting of schools was undertaken to make them earthquake resistant. Also in post- earthquake reconstruction programmes retrofitting was incorporated. Trainings of Engineers, contractors, craftsmen and local government officials on earthquake resistance in school building were conducted. Safety drills and information on earthquake preparedness was imparted. Similar initiatives were undertaken in Bangdung, Indonesia where awareness and training programmes on earthquake safety were conducted.

This is a significant departure from the traditional approach (where humanitarian assistance and relief is provided only after a disaster takes place to address the stress and shock) and aims to minimize disaster risk (addressing the root cause) before the disaster strikes.

Paradigm shift in India: In India, the worldwide attention on IDNDR resulted in concern over the huge developmental losses from disasters, which a country like India could barely afford. A series of disasters like the Uttarkashi Earthquake 1991, Latur Earthquake 1993, Jabalpur Earthquake 1997, Malpa Landslide 1998, Chamoli Earthquake of 1999, Orissa Supercyclone of 1999 followed by the Bhuj Earthquake of 2001 hit the country during this time causing the general thinking to shift towards a prevention and mitigation regime. The need to prevent such devastation from happening by preparing in advance began to gain prominence.

This felt need result in some concrete mitigation actions like preparation of the Vulnerability Atlas of India, establishment of training and capacity building facilities on disaster management at the Centre and states, upgradation of early warning system etc. The High Powered Committee (HPC) on Disaster set up in 1999 focused on the need for a holistic effort, considering all disasters within a coordinated system of governance. The HPC also focused on instilling a Culture of Prevention. The Tenth Five Year Plan also added a separate chapter on Disaster Management - The Development Perspective "with the objective to inform, guide and provide specific strategies to all State Government in disaster management".

The last two devastating calamities viz the Bhuj Earthquake 2001 and the Asian Tsunami 2004 gave a momentum to this paradigm shift because it focused on the fact that the apparent loss of human life, assets and property hides insurmountable losses in livelihood, social capital and economic development. The cost of rehabilitation and reconstruction of a shattered infrastructure and economy are indeed enormous, carried over for years. The hard facts that showed how the nation was losing the gains of development with average annual deaths of 4350 people, 40000 animals, damage of 2.5 million houses and crop loss over 1.5 million hectares, accounting for 2.25% of Gross Domestic Product (GDP).

A comprehensive framework for disaster management was then developed in a multi-sectoral and multi-disciplinary format. This approach proceeds from the conviction that development cannot be sustainable unless disaster mitigation is built into the development process and investments in mitigation are much more cost-effective than expenditure on relief and rehabilitation. The underlying premise within which this framework has been formulated is that while hazards are inevitable, they need not convert into disasters every time. Another corner stone of the approach is that mitigation has to be multi-disciplinary spanning across all sectors of development. A coordinated mechanism of preparedness, prevention, response and rehabilitation involving all stakeholders would be instrumental in bringing about the Culture of Prevention. One of the most significant changes was brought about through a Central legislation on disaster management.

Q11. Briefly describe the Disaster Management Act, 2005. Also describe the mandates of the Act at the national, state and district levels.

Ans. The Disaster Management Act, 2005 was passed by the Rajya Sabha, the upper house of the Parliament of India on 28 November, and the Lok Sabha, the lower house of the Parliament, on 12 December 2005. It received the assent of The President of India on 23 December 2005. The Disaster Management Act, 2005 has 11 chapters and 79 sections. The Act extends to the whole of India. The Act provides for "the effective management of disasters and for matters connected there with or incidental thereto." The main focus of this act is to provide the people who are affected with disasters, their life back and helping them.

The Act defines disaster management as "a continuous and integrated process of planning, organizing, coordinating and implementing measures which are necessary or expedient for:

- prevention of danger or threat of any danger.
- mitigation or reduction of risk of any disaster or its severity or consequences.
- capacity building.
- preparedness to deal with any disaster.
- prompt response to any threatening disaster situation or disaster.
- assessing the severity or magnitude of effects of any disaster
- evacuation, rescue and relief.
- rehabilitation and reconstruction.

The DM Act 2005 is an attempt at setting up and institutionalising a dedicated system for disaster management. To this end, it mandates the setting up of key institutions at the national, state and district levels. The Act aimed towards creating a hierarchy of institutions for policy and planning, implementation, capacity building, response force, thereby ensuring a holistic effort towards disaster management. By setting up specific institutions, the Act has cleared the uncertainty regarding the exact division of responsibilities and duties between various tiers of government.

Mandates of the DM Act – Institutional Mechanism at the National Level: The Disaster Management Act 2005 has created a hierarchy of institutions at the national, state and district levels for holistic management of disasters. In doing so, the Act has formally abandoned the earlier notion that disaster management is the sole responsibility of the states with the Central Government only playing a supportive role. The definite role of Central Government is ensured through the formation of a number of organizations at the Central level. The national level organizations created as per the Act are:

- **National Disaster Management Authority (NDMA):** The Act calls for the establishment of National Disaster Management Authority (NDMA), with the Prime Minister of India as chairperson. The NDMA may have no more than nine members including a Vice-Chairperson. The tenure of the members of the NDMA shall be five years. The NDMA which was initially established on 30 May 2005 by an executive order, was constituted under Section-3(1) of the Disaster Management Act, on 27 September 2006. The NDMA is responsible for "laying down the policies, plans and guidelines for disaster management" and to ensure "timely and effective response to disaster". Under section 6 of the Act it is responsible for laying "down guidelines to be followed by the State Authorities in drawing up the State Plans".
- **National Executive Committee (NEC):** The Act under Section 8 enjoins the Central Government to Constitute a National Executive Committee (NEC) to assist the National Authority. The NEC is composed of Secretary level officers of the Government of India in the Ministries of home, agriculture, atomic energy, defence, drinking water supply, environment and forests, finance (expenditure), health, power, rural development, science and technology, space, telecommunication, urban development, and water resources, with the Home secretary serving as the Chairperson, ex officio. The Chief of the Integrated Defence Staff of the Chiefs of Staff Committee, is an ex officio member of the NEC. The NEC under section of the Act is responsible for the preparation of the National Disaster Management Plan for the whole country and to ensure that it is "reviewed and updated annually".

- **National Institute of Disaster Management (NIDM):** NIDM was founded from its predecessor National Centre for Disaster Management (NCDM) with an aim of creating an Institute of excellence in disaster management studies in India. As per provisions of the Act, NIDM is required to design, develop and implement training programmes, undertake research, formulated and implement a comprehensive human resource development plan, provide assistance in national policy formulation, assist other research and training institutes, state governments and other organizations for successfully discharging their responsibilities, develop educational materials for dissemination and promote awareness among stakeholders in addition to undertake any other functions as assigned to it by the Central Government. NIDM is also required to network with various research and training institutions for sharing of knowledge and resources.
- **National Disaster Response Force:** The Section 44–45 of the Act provides for constituting a National Disaster Response Force "for the purpose of specialist response to a threatening disaster situation or disaster" under a Director General to be appointed by the Central Government. In September 2014 Kashmir-floods NDRF along with the armed forces played a vital role in rescuing the locals and tourists, for which NDRF was awarded by the government of India.

Mandates of the DM Act - Institutional Mechanism at the State Level: A similar institutional structure has been created at the State level with each state to have the following set up:

- **State Disaster Management Authorities (SDMA):** State Disaster management Authorities under the chairpersonship of the Chief Minister are mandated by the Act for laying down disaster management plans and policies of the state, coordinate implementation, lay down guidelines, recommend provision of funds for mitigation and preparedness review the measures taken for preparedness, mitigation and disaster risk reduction. 23 states have already notified their SDMAs.
- **State Executive Committee:** The State Government is empowered to constitute the State Executive Committee under

the chairpersonship of the Chief Secretary and four secretaries of relevant departments. This Committee is responsible for implementing the national Plan and the State Plan and act as the coordinating and monitoring body for management of disasters in the state. The Committee will prepare the State Disaster Management Plan as per the guidelines laid down by the National Authority after consultation with local authorities, departments and people's representatives, as the Committee may deem fit.

- **State Disaster Response Forces (SDRFs):** The state have been advised to set up their own Specialist Response Forces for disaster response. The existing resources of the state armed police, fire and rescue services, Home Guards, Civil Defence, etc., would be the sources from which the SDRFs may be constituted to generate specialist response. They will also include women members for looking after the needs of women and children. NDRF battalions and their training institutions will assist the state/UTs in this effort.

Mandates of the DM Act - Institutional Mechanism at the District Level: Most of the disaster management initiatives are operationalized at the district level. Recognizing the need to create a strong implementing and coordinating body at the district level the Act has provided for the creation of a District Disaster Management Authority (DDMA) in each of the six hundred plus districts of the country.

District Disaster Management Authorities: Every state will constitute a District Disaster Management Authority under the co-chairpersonship of the District Magistrate and the President of the Zilla Parishad, providing for integration of the executive and legislative focal points at the district level. The District Disaster Management Authorities shall act as the district planning, coordinating and implementing body for disaster management. Their major responsibilities would include inter alia:

- preparation of district disaster management plan including district response plan,
- coordination and monitoring implementation of the national and state policies and plans and

- to take requisite measure for-disaster prevention and mitigation in the vulnerable areas of the district.
- to give directions to concerned departments for putting in place risk reduction measures,
- to organize capacity building of the staff,
- to facilitate community training and awareness,
- to coordinate early warning and dissemination mechanisms,
- to establish stockpiles of relief and rescue materials
- to ensure regular rehearsals, drills etc. and
- communicating with their State Authority for effective disaster management. The process of notifying the District Authorities is currently under way in most states.

Q12. What are the mandates of DM Act in respect of financial provision?

Or

Elucidate the mandates of disaster management act for financial provisions.

Ans. The financial provisions of the Act are in keeping with the underlying aim of addressing disaster risk reduction through effective response and sustained prevention and mitigation measures in a holistic framework. The Act has made clear demarcations between response and mitigation funding, thereby acknowledging the inherent difference between expenditure needs for response during disaster situations and those of mitigation during normal times.

- **National Funds:** the DM Act has provided for two funds viz. National Disaster Response Fund and National Disaster Mitigation Fund. The National Disaster Response Fund, as specified in the Act, would be used for "meeting any threatening disaster situation or disaster." The Fund will comprise of two components, the majority from a corpus deposited by the Government and any other grants, donations made by any person or institution for the purpose of disaster management. The Response Fund would be available with the National Executive Committee, who would use it towards meeting the expenses for emergency response, relief and rehabilitation according to the guidelines laid down by the Government, in consultation with the National Authority.

The National Disaster Mitigation Fund has been provided exclusively for the purpose of mitigation and would be used only for mitigation projects. The corpus of the fund would be provided by the Central Government after due appropriation made by Parliament, by law, This fund would be applied by the National Authority

- **State Funds:** Similar funds are to be provided at the state and district levels. The Act enjoins the State Governments to create Response and Mitigation Funds at the state and district levels. The State Disaster Response Fund, available with the State Executive Committee, would available for emergency response, relief and rehabilitation at the state level, while the State Disaster Mitigation Fund, to be made available to the State Disaster Management Authority for mitigation projects.
- **District Funds:** At the district level, the State Government has to create similar funds for the district level. The District Disaster Response Fund and the District Disaster Mitigation Fund would be made available to the District Authorities for response and mitigation purposes respectively.

Feedback is the breakfast of Champions.

Ken Blanchard

You can Help other students.
"Inform any error or mistake in this book."

We and Universe
will reward you for Your Kind act.

Email at : feedback@gullybaba.com
or
WhatsApp on 9350849407

Chapter-2

Mitigation and Preparedness

Q1. Explain the concept of community based disaster management. Explain its importance.

Or

What is community based disaster management (CBDM)? Discuss the need and importance of CBDM.

Ans. Community Based Disaster Management (CBDM) initiates a process involving sequential stages that can be operationalized to reduce disaster risk. Processes of CBDM are guided by principles of subsidiarity, economies of scale, equity, heterogeneity, and public accountability. The different stages in CBDM are disaster/vulnerability risk assessment, risk reduction planning, early warning systems, post-disaster relief, and participatory monitoring and evaluation.

CBDM by its very nature demands a decentralized bottoms-up approach with intensive, micro interventions at the local Panchayats, ward or village level with the intention of generating confidence, awareness, knowledge, partnership, and ownership for planning and rolling out local disaster management plans encompassing all levels of disaster management continuum.

Need or Importance of CBDM: The rationale for involving communities in disaster preparedness and mitigation activities is based on the following assumptions:

- Communities in disaster affected areas are the real sufferers and are the first responders as well.

- Communities in high risk areas have often developed their own coping mechanisms and strategies to reduce the impact of disaster. It is important to appreciate this local knowledge and resources, and to build on them in order to improve the capacity of the people to withstand the impact of disasters.
- Ownership of disaster reduction should not be stripped from local people who would be left even more powerless in case external intervention does not occur.
- Disaster reduction activities should be based on participatory approaches involving local communities as much as possible, considering them as proactive stakeholders and not passive targets for intervention.
- Involvement and participation of the communities will ensure a collective and coordinated action during emergencies.
- Building community leadership and a chain of trained community cadres through participatory approach can help harness the resilience and resourcefulness of the community to cope.
- Solution is sustainable if it comes from people themselves rather than thrusting upon them.

Q2. Elaborate the various components of community based disaster management (CBDM).

Or

What are the various components of community based disaster management (CBDM)?

Ans. The various Components of CBDM Include:

- **Community Profile:** This includes the community characteristics including its physical, administrative, geographic, demographic, socio economic, and infrastructure profile. Its development position and the context upon which disaster will impact the area, should also be included in the profile
- **Resource Inventory:** Involves analyzing the local resources available within the community, which can be harnessed and enhanced for disaster preparedness and response. It shall include a listing of trained manpower, livelihood activities,

health, education, water, sanitation, electricity, communications, and transport facilities. It shall also include information a local committee task forces and emergency directory.

- **Risk map through Community Maps:** This shall include the Open spaces, Medical Facilities, Communication Facilities, Transportation Facilities, Water Facilities, Temporary Shelters, Sanitation Facilities, and Search and Rescue Operation facilities.
- **Future Mock drill:** this is a list of dates when the periodic mock drill in the community will be conducted.

In case the unit of community is taken as a village, then development of Village Disaster Management Plan (VDMP) by the community ensures ownership and reflects local conditions.

The village disaster management plan is a document which details out the past hazard profile of a village and the present vulnerability statues on the basis of which we can prepare to prevent future hazards from becoming disasters. The plan is essentially a preparedness tool which can be used during an emergency by the administration as well as the community to have an insight into the location of available men and material local resources in the village. The VDMP must have the following features:

- Have a clearly stated objective or set of objectives.
- Reflect a systematic sequence or activities in a logical and clear manner.
- Assign specific tasks and responsibilities.
- Integrate its activities, tasks and responsibilities to enable the overall objective or series of objectives to be achieved.

A VDMP can prove to be beneficial as:

- It can be used to tap men and material resources in the aftermath of a disaster.
- It lists down the contact details of important administrative officials ensuring quick communication with the administration officials.
- It describe the roles and responsibilities of the concerned official and teams in the wake of a disaster.

Framework for VDMP: The framework for VDMP involves the following steps:

Step 1: Village Profile: The village profile would include information like population, geographical area, temperature, rainfall, agricultural land, cropping pattern, education, economy, occupation, literacy rate, income, rivers, road, industries, hospitals, schools, temples, sex ratio, families below poverty line, livelihood pattern, drinking water sources, critical establishments and other critical infrastructure.

The community may be asked to draw a map depicting the location of pucca and kutcha houses, livelihood of people, forests and trees, tanks and ponds, tube wells, public health services, drinking water facilities, telephone installations, road and railway infrastructure, post office, temples, school, shelters etc.

Step 2: Hazard Analysis: It refers to prioritizing disasters based on its frequency and analysis of the estimated losses. This can be carried out by taking the help of elderly people of the village. The villagers analyze the losses that they had incurred during various disasters and learn the best practices carried out. This is an important activity as its forms the basis for preparedness and mitigation plans.

The community would be asked to review and analyze the occurrence of past disasters and hazards. Group discussions along with the elderly population, teachers and children can be held focusing on the disasters and hazards faced by the community for the past one year to past fifteen years, kind and nature of disasters and hazards faced, experience in the last hazard faced, warning issued, damage caused, response to the disaster, relief and rehabilitation process, traditional methods of coping of the community, gaps in management of the hazard, lessons learnt. It can be useful in understanding the nature, intensity and behavior of the past disasters and hazards.

The community may be asked to identity both natural as well as human made hazards. Natural hazards may include floods, drought, earthquake, cyclone, sandstorm, cloudburst etc. human made hazards for the community may include industrial and chemical accidents, road and railway accidents, fire, epidemic, building collapse, communal violence etc.

Step 3: Vulnerability Assessment: The process would involve asking the community two major questions namely;

- Who is vulnerable?
- What is vulnerable?

The community would be asked to identify the more vulnerable population, identify the location of women (pregnant, lactating, widows, single), children, elderly, physically challenged, mentally challenged, those dependent on life support systems and medicines, poor people living by the sea or kutcha houses, livestock and cattle etc. The community would also be asked to identify the vulnerable infrastructure like kutcha houses, low lying areas, areas near the water bodies such as the sea and river and direction of wind, livelihood assets such as boats and nets, documents, weak structures, drinking water resources, communication lines roads, telephone lines etc.

Step 4: Resource Analysis: Resource analysis focuses on identifying locally available assets and resources that can be utilized for building the capacities of the community during and after disasters. The local community has a lot of inbuilt strength and capacity for handling the disasters. It is important to capture the capacity and strength of the community in resource analysis. Apart from infrastructure and funds, it could be individuals with specific skills, local institutions and people's knowledge as all these have the capacity to create awareness and bring about changes in the community. Resource analysis is therefore not limited to a map depicting the available resources but also plotting of the distribution, access and its use by taking into consideration prevailing sensitiveness the village. Thus assessment of resources would involve two components:

- Human Resource Assessment
- Material Resource Assessment

The process would involve identifying safe houses and building for shelter, strong building, elevated uplands and structures, safe evacuation routes, health, medical and sanitation facilities, swimmers, doctors, nurses, sources of funds to carry out preparedness activities, volunteers for task etc.

Step 5: Risk Assessment: On the basis of hazard, vulnerability and resource analysis, the community is asked to determine and rank the hazards posing the highest as well as the lowest risk. The community also explores the reasons why a particular hazard poses the highest risk on the basis of the vulnerability and resource analysis.

Step 6: Response Plan: The onset of an emergency the need for time sensitive actions to save life and property, reduce hardships and suffering, and restore essential life support and community systems. Effective response planning requires realistic identification of likely response functions, assignment of specific tasks to individual response teams and agencies, identification of equipment, supplies and personnel required by the response agencies for performing the assigned tasks. A response plan should be backed by proper Standard operating procedure for disaster management committees and teams. The response plan should focus on the following:

- Operational direction and coordination
- Emergency warning and dissemination
- Rapid damage assessment and reporting
- Search and rescue
- Medical response
- Logistic arrangements
- Communication
- Temporary shelter management
- Law and order

Step 7: Reconstruction and Recovery Plan: This aspect of the plan should focus on the restoration of normalcy to the lives and livelihoods of the affected population. The reconstruction of infrastructure should follow the principle of "build back better". Short-term recovery aims at restoration of vital life support systems to minimum operating standards, while long term rehabilitation continues till complete redevelopment of the area takes place. Recovery and Reconstruction Plan should take into account the following components:

- Restoration of basic infrastructure.
- Reconstruction/repair of lifeline buildings/social infrastructure.
- Reconstruction/repair of damaged buildings.
- Restoration of livelihoods.
- Physical and Mental Medical Rehabilitation.

Step 8: Mitigation Plan: The plan should focus on reducing the impacts of disasters on the communities through damage prevention. The main focus may be given to disaster mitigation owing to its importance in reducing the losses. The mitigation plans should be specific for different kinds of hazards identified in the HRVC analysis section. Mitigation plans should deal with both aspects: structural and non-structural. Identification of various departments including Panchayat Raj Institutions for implementing the mitigation strategies is important. Community mitigation measures should be identified and implementation modalities formulated. The mitigation plan should also include a section on preparedness planning. Some indicative components may include:

- Operational readiness of facilities, equipment and stores.
- Setting up of infrastructure, communication etc.
- Updation of resource inventory, before the flood/cyclone season.
- Management/skills/simulation training.
- Community awareness

Step 9: Contact Details: At the end of the plan contact details of personnel who are involved in the management of the disaster should be listed out like of village panchayat officials, village development officer, village task force, emergency resource owners, swimmers, members of the disaster management committees, members of various disaster management teams, local NGO's etc.

Disaster Management Committees and Teams have to be formed at the village level to facilitate the process of Community-Based Disaster Preparedness. The disaster management committees can plan the process of disaster management in the village while teams may be constituted to carry out important tasks like issuance of warning, evacuation and response, first aid, damage assessment, water and sanitation, carcass disposal, shelter management, psycho-social counseling, relief management and rehabilitation. There is a strong need for setting up DMCs in the village to carry out the following functions:

(1) To take village level decisions,

(2) To coordinate the activities of the Disaster management Teams,

(3) To account for and to maintain the inventory of Community-based Disaster preparedness materials,

(4) To able to ensure a continuous monitoring of preparedness.

Mock Drills have to be conducted at regular intervals on the basis of plan prepared by the community. The mock drills will be a form of rehearsal in which the response of the community and the efficacy of the administration will be tested. The mock drill will also test the applicability of the village disaster management plan.

Awareness has to be generated amongst the community through various mediums like televisions, radio and print media. These campaigns are carried out through rallies, street plays, competitions in schools, distribution of IEC materials, wall paintings on do's and don'ts for various hazards. Meetings with key persons of a village such as the village head, health worker, school teachers, elected representatives and members of the youth clubs and women also motivate the villagers to carry forward these plans for a safer living.

Training is an integral component of CBDM. The important stakeholders like PRIs, Village volunteers, Disaster Management Committees, Disaster Management Teams have to be trained so that they can lead the process of disaster management in their community and make it as a way of their life.

Community Contingency Fund is a vital component of CBDM. Availability of resources for various activities to be carried at different phases of the cycle is very crucial. Even though initial resources may be provided by an external agency, it is mandatory that the community participates in resource generation and funding of the entire Community-Based Disaster Preparedness exercise. This is the greatest indicator of involvement and thereby ownership. Participation can take two forms, both monetary cash and donations and non-monetary i.e. goods, labour, usage of community goods such as plantations. To allow for the maintenance of the structures created and to allow the community to keep itself up to date in Community-Based Disaster Preparedness by the way of drills, a Community Contingency Fund (CCF) needs to be set up. A very nominal amount based on the affording capacity of the inhabitants (households) should be collected and kept as the Community Contingency Fund or village emergency fund. Additional sources can be governmental or non-governmental grants, income from community property such as ponds, plantations, and usage of the shelter on a temporary rental basis for events such as marriages, rental income from a school etc.

Q3. What is the role of community in disaster management?

Or

Discuss the role of community in disaster management.

Ans. Community plays a vital role in reducing the impact of a disaster. People at this level are often the most vulnerable to disaster and experience the greatest impacts for various reasons. With knowledge of the local geology, the hazard context, and the livelihoods options available, local communities must be involved in disaster management programmes from the start. As it is often the same group of people that are affected worst by disasters and climate change, the community-based approach outlined here is a useful tool for adaptation. Disasters only occur when a hazard arises in vulnerable conditions. Hazards occurring in uninhabited areas or in areas where economic activities and settlement patterns are not vulnerable do not cause disasters.

During Disaster: The community can play a vital role in the following stages during a disaster:

- Search & Rescue.
- Evacuation.
- Medical First Response.
- Building and locating place for temporary shelters.
- Needs analysis of the affected community.
- Relief Management and Distribution.
- Identification of Vulnerable Groups'.
- Coordination with authorities/NGOs.
- Reduces costs as it uses local material and wisdom.

After a Disaster: The community can also play an important role in the rehabilitation and recovery phase where existing local coping strategies can be used for the maximum benefit as it:

- Reduces costs as it uses local material and wisdom
- Serves in Long-term Mitigation
- Helps in restoration of affected livelihoods and economy

Before a Disaster: The community can play a pivotal role in mitigation and preparedness of a disaster. Some of the activities in which the community can be roped in are as follows:

- Identification of the vulnerable areas.

- Identification of the vulnerable population.
- Aware of the past history.
- Making Disaster Management Plans.
- Local coping strategies.
- Awareness Generation.
- Community-Based Warning System.

Q4. Explain the linkage of development planning with community based disaster management (CBDM).

Ans. The Community-Based Disaster Management need to be integrated with varied development plans and regulations launched by the government as well as NGO's for effective mitigation of disasters. Development activities that do not considers the disaster loss perspective fail to be sustainable. The compounded costs of disasters relating to loss of life, loss of assets, economic activities, and cost of reconstruction of not only assets but of lives can scarcely be borne by any community or nation. Therefore, all development schemes in vulnerable areas should include a disaster mitigation analysis, whereby the feasibility of a project is assessed with respect to vulnerability of the area and the mitigation measures required for sustainability. Environmental protection, afforestation programmes, pollution control, construction of earthquake resistant structures etc., should therefore have high priority within the plans.

Developmental Schemes that inculcate disaster mitigations: Some of the schemes that are being run in various areas which incorporate an element of disaster mitigation are as follows:

- Integrated Wasteland Development Programme (IWDP)
- Drought Prone Area Programme (DPAP)
- Desert Development Programme (DDP)
- Flood Control Programmes
- National Afforestation & Eco-development Programme (NA&ED)
- Accelerated Rural Water Supply Programme (ARWSP)
- Crop Insurance Schemes
- Sampurn Grammen Rozgar Yojana (SGRY)
- Food for work etc.

Integration of the development schemes with Disaster Mitigation: The aim of development in any area should be safer development for the community of the area. For this, all development projects in that village or area should be sensitive towards disaster mitigation. It makes good economic sense to spend a little extra today in a planned way on steps and components that can help in prevention and mitigation of disasters, than to spend much more later on relief, restoration and rehabilitation. The design of development projects and the process of development should take the aspect of disaster reduction and mitigation within its purview; otherwise, the development does not sustain with time and gets washed away as soon as a hazard strikes the area.

Q5. What are the major challenges faced in the process of CBDM.

Or

Elaborate the issues which are faced in the process of CBDM.

Ans. Some of the issues and challenges faced in the process are as follows:

(1) NGOs try a variety of means to build community capacity in preparedness, mitigation, and response, without any tested and accepted models.

(2) The results of these efforts are generally neither been will monitored nor the impact well measured. Minimal interagency learning takes place.

(3) There is an immediate need to standardize practices, with local government, local NGOs, and communities affected by disasters.

(4) There is an absence of generally accepted standards for community participation in emergencies.

(5) It is often difficult to sustain the motivation and preparedness level of the communities, in a situation where the larger sections of civil society, government, media and general public remain immune to the need for internalizing the culture of disaster prevention and preparedness.

(6) Another challenge lies in the establishment, consolidation and empowerment of similar structures at provincial, district and local levels.

(7) Various organisations in the country are carrying out CBDP programmes in isolation and with a project mode. This creates the risk of duplication of efforts and the community initiative ceases as soon the project ends.

(8) The process of institutionalising the training of DMT's is not focused upon or looked into. Consequently, many task forces become defunct after the project closes.

Q6. Discuss the following case studies related to community based disaster management:

(i) Great Hanshin earthquake

Ans. The Great Hanshin earthquake or Kobe earthquake, occurred on January 17, 1995 in the southern part of Hyōgo Prefecture, Japan, when combined with Osaka, known as Hanshin. It measured 6.9 on the moment magnitude scale and 7 on the JMA Shindo intensity scale. The tremors lasted for approximately 20 seconds. The focus of the earthquake was located 17 km beneath its epicenter, on the northern end of Awaji Island, 20 km away from the center of the city of Kobe.

Up to 6,434 people lost their lives; about 4,600 of them were from Kobe. Among major cities, Kobe, with its population of 1.5 million, was the closest to the epicenter and hit by the strongest tremors. This was Japan's worst earthquake in the 20th century after the Great Kantō earthquake in 1923, which claimed more than 105,000 lives.

Among some 35,000 people who suffered difficulties in evacuating themselves, 77 percent were rescued by their neighbours, 19 percent by the rescue workers and 4 percent by others. The case study highlighted the need to train the community in search and rescue techniques so that many more lives can be saved at the time of disasters.

(ii) Latur earthquake

Ans. The 1993 Latur earthquake struck India at 3:56 am local time on 30 September. The main area affected was Maharashtra State in Western India. The earthquake primarily affected the districts of Latur and Osmanabad, including the Ausa block of Latur and Omerga of Osmanabad. Fifty-two villages were demolished in the intraplate earthquake. It measured 6.2 on the moment magnitude scale, and approximately 10,000 people died, whilst another 30,000 were injured. The earthquake's hypocenter was around 10 km deep – relatively shallow – allowing shock waves to cause more damage.

After the earthquake, the government built houses for rehabilitating the community. They built typical "suburban house" which were alien and unsuitable for the rural lifestyle. The houses had lesser space to accommodate grain storage bins and traditional machines of the weavers.

There was no place for the wood-fire smoke to escape, making the interior black. The houses were located very far way from the fields. Moreover, the social life of the community was also disturbed as people close to one another were relocated at different parts. The community did not accept these houses. They discarded them as they were not involved in planning of these houses. The government learnt its lesson and later involved the community in planning and building houses. The houses were finally accepted by the affected community as the new houses were sensitive to the rural lifestyle. The Latur earthquake highlighted the need to involve the community in rehabilitation process.

(iii) Khanna rail disaster

Ans. The Khanna rail disaster occurred on 26 November 1998 near Khanna on the Khanna-Ludhiana section of India's Northern Railway in Punjab, at 03:15 when the Calcutta-bound Jammu Tawi-Sealdah Express collided with six derailed coaches of the Amritsar-bound "Frontier Mail" which were lying in its path. At least 212 were killed; in total the trains were estimated to be carrying 2,500 passengers. The initial derailment was caused by a broken rail.

The local community rose to the occasion and responded to this exigency in the wee hours of the cold morning. The local gurudwara used the mikes to awaken the people of the village asked them to help. The villagers lined up their tractors, started the engines and switched on the headlights to facilitate the rescue operations. Some of them also burnt bundles of paddy straw to warm the atmosphere and save the injured people from biting cold. The local Gurudwara turned into a medical camp and food cooked in langar was served to them while the help from administration reached by 6 am in the morning. The case study highlights the vital role of community in disaster response.

(iv) Drought in Bhilwara

Ans. The community started a Community Pasture Development Programme in drought prone Bhilwara district of Rajasthan for growing fodder for the livestock on the community Pasture land. The community pasture land was cordoned off by making trench cum mounds followed by a live hedge, using a popular fence plant locally known as Thor (Euphorbia). Seeds of Dhaman grass were sown after tilling the land by a tractor top ensures groundcover. The community members arranged seed collection, and decided that all the families in the village could cut the grass and deposit 50% with the committee, which was later, sold to the needy members at a low cost. Apart from the sale of grass and fodder seeds the community members also decided amongst themselves to permit the members to cut thin branches of the trees for fodder and fuel wood. The average income generated from the community pastures was between ₹2500–4500 per hectare, out of which 80–85% was contributed by the sale of the grass and the rest by the sale of seeds, fine one stray cattle etc.

Q7. Define early warning system. Point out its major elements.

Or

What are the various elements of early warning system?

Ans. The early warning system can be understand as an integrated system of hazard monitoring, forecasting and prediction, disaster risk assessment, communication and preparedness activities systems and processes that enables individuals, communities, governments, businesses and others to take timely action to reduce disaster risks in advance of hazardous events.

An Early Warning System (EWS) can be defined as a set of capacities needed to generate and disseminate timely and meaningful warning information of the possible extreme events or disasters (e.g. floods, drought, fire, earthquake and tsunamis) that threatens people's lives. The purpose of this information is to enable individuals, communities and organizations threatened to prepare and act appropriately and in sufficient time to reduce the possibility of harm, loss or risk.

Elements of Early warning: Early warning is the integration of four main elements:

- **Risk Knowledge:** Risk assessment provides essential information to set priorities for mitigation and prevention strategies and designing early warning systems.
- **Monitoring and Predicting:** Systems with monitoring and predicting capabilities provide timely estimates of the potential risk faced by communities, economies and the environment.
- **Disseminating Information:** Communication systems are needed for delivering warning messages to the potentially affected locations to alert local and regional governmental agencies. The messages need to be reliable, synthetic and simple to be understood by authorities and public.

- **Response:** Coordination, good governance and appropriate action plans are a key point in effective early warning. Likewise, public awareness and education are critical aspects of disaster mitigation.

Q8. Describe the early warning system for Cyclone, Tsunami and Flood.

Or

What are the various early warning systems adopted by various disaster management authorities?

Ans. Early warning system for various disasters are as follows:

(1) Flood Warning Systems in India: Flood forecasting and warning systems in India, consists of structural flood management measures such as embankments and channels, which aim at minimizing flood damage and also better planning of rescue/relief operations. Scientific Flood Forecasting in India is with 173 flood forecasting stations in nine major river systems, and 71 river sub-basins in 15 states. The Central Water Commission (CWC) is in charge of these systems. For other intra-state rivers, states have to establish such systems, usually they are not in place.

Each year, CWC issues nearly 6,000 forecasts during the flood season, usually 12 to 48 hours in advance. For this, CWC has hydrological data from 700 Gauge and Discharge sites and hydro-meteorological data over 500 rain gauge stations, through a network of about 550 wireless stations. IMD provides synoptic weather reports, weather forecast/heavy rainfall warnings etc., to CWC. Flood forecasting systems have received support in each Five year Plan, to improve the systems needed, to issue more accurate and timely warnings.

(2) Cyclone Warning Systems: The India Meteorological Department (IMD), follows a four-stage warning system for issuing warnings for tropical cyclones. A "Pre-cyclone Watch" is issued whenever a depression forms over the Bay of Bengal or Arabian Sea, followed by a "Cyclone Alert", issued 2-3 days in advance of commencement of bad weather along the coast. In the third stage, Cyclone Warnings are issued 1-2 days in advance, which specify the expected place and time of landfall of the tropical cyclone. The final stage is known as "postlandfall Outlook", which is issued 12 hours in advanced of landfall and contains location specific forecast of landfall along with other warning details. The

Cyclone Warning Organization in India has a 3-tier system to cater to the needs of the maritime States. These are:

- Cyclone Warning Division (CWD) set up at IMD Head Quarters to co-ordinate and supervise cyclone warning operations in the country and to advise the Govt. at the apex level;
- Area Cyclone Warning Centres (ACWC) at Chennai, Mumbai and Kolkata and
- Cyclone Warning Centres at Visakhapatnam, Ahmedabad and Bhubaneswar.

The cyclone warning work is also supervised and coordinated by the Forecasting Division at Pune.

With new observation systems such as buoys, Doppler Radars and new generation satellites, these forecasts are likely to improve further. Five Doppler Weather Radars (DWRs) have started functioning along the east coast at Visakapattinam, Kolkata, Machilipatnam, Chennai and Sriharikota.

(iii) Tsunami Warning Systems: Tsunami is a system of ocean gravity waves formed as a result of large-scale disturbance of the sea floor that occurs in a relatively short duration of time. The Indian Ocean is likely to be affected by tsunamis generated mainly by earthquakes from the two potential source regions, the Andaman-Nicobar-Sumatra Island Arc and the Makran Subduction Zone. A state-of-the-art warning centre has been established at INCOIS with all the necessary computational and communication infrastructure that enables reception of real-time data from the network of national and international seismic stations, tide gauges and bottom pressure recorders (BPRs). Earthquake parameters are computed in the less than 15 minutes of occurrence. A database of pre-run scenarios for travel times and run-up-height has been created using Tsunami N2 model. At the time of event, the closest scenario is picked from the database for generating advisories. Water level data enables confirmation or cancellation of a tsunami. Tsunami bulletins are then generated based on decision support rules and disseminated to the concerned authorities for action, following a standard operating procedure. The criteria for generation of advisories (warning/alert/watch) are based on the tsunamigenic potential of an earthquake, travel time (i.e. time taken by the tsunami wave to reach the particular coast) and likely inundation. The performance of the system was tested on September 12, 2007 earthquake of magnitude 8.4 off Java coast. The system performed as designed. It was possible to generate advisories in time for the administration and possible evacuation was avoided.

Q9. What are the basic features of early warning?

Ans. Early warning is a major element of disaster risk reduction. It prevents loss of life and reduces the economic and material impact of disasters. To be effective, early warning systems need to actively involve the communities at risk, facilitate public education and awareness of risks, effectively disseminate messages and warnings and ensure there is constant state of preparedness. Some of the key features of early warning are given below:

- **Source of the Warning:** A warning source is the entity or agency responsible for initiating warning communication and it can be government agencies, media figures, or friends and relatives etc. Warning originating from credible sources is likely to promote warning compliances. Further, the population warned will be normally heterogeneous and there will be different sub groups such population who will receive warning from different sources. These sources may have varying credibility and trustworthiness and accordingly there may be difference in response.
- **Warning Message:** A warning message should provide some basic information such as date and time of issues, source, validity period of warning, targeted audience for whom the warning is intended, location of phenomena and the likely impact areas, recommended protective action, availability of the next warning-time, source etc. In general terms, the warning message should describe about who should do, what, when, how, with whom, why and with what consequences. Clarity of the message and specificity are important attributes attached to early warning. For example, it may not be sufficient to say simply that a dam will break. To facilities response it must give the height and speed of impact of flood water that will ensue, size and location of the area that can be affected. Certainty and accuracy is generally sought in warning

message, however in some cases it may not be possible to provide fully accurate forecast due to several factors such as lack of scientific data, inadequate understanding of the phenomena etc. Another important feature of early warning message is that it should be consistent both internally and externally.

- **Warning Communication Channels:** Warning can be communicated through broadly voice, signals or printed mediums. Voice can be direct like personal notification for example telephone, door to door, very high frequency radio etc. or indirect such as broadcast over radio, television etc. These mediums have their inherent strengths and weaknesses for example radio or television warning will find it difficult to warn a much selected audience, similarly signals have to be interpreted correctly. Permanent warning signs or sirens/alarms are sometimes used for remote locations and in such case people must be made aware about meaning of these signs and sirens and what to do during such times. Often more than one channel is used for early warning and the choice of a channel or channel mix should depend on the hazard under consideration and characteristics of population to be warned. The selection of channel should consider factors such as amount of information needed to communicate the hazard risk, amount of information each channel is capable of carrying and time available.
- **Frequency of Warning**: Frequency or the number of times a warning should be repeated is best dictated by the need of the situation. The frequency should be ideally geared to the dynamics of emerging risk and severity. During any warning phase, people constantly want updates on the risk even when there is little change in the hazard status.
- **Receive Characteristics:** The public response to early warning varies and depends on a number of factors and the information contained in warning interacts with various personal attributes of recipient. These include warning belief or determining that a threat exist, sense of personal risk or to what extent the predicted event will affect individuals, family etc. When

people receive a disaster warning their perception of risk is often shaped by their pre-existing beliefs in the likelihood of its occurrence. Similarly, the characteristics of the disaster agent can have significant influence on public response. People can have different level of awareness and familiarisation about various hazards and prior experience of a hazard can affect individuals' assessment of the risk and pre-disposes their likelihood of taking a protective action.

Q10. What is mitigation? Discuss the various goals of mitigation.

Ans. Mitigation is the reduction of something harmful or the reduction of its harmful effects. It may refer to measures taken to reduce the harmful effects of hazards that remain in potentia, or to manage harmful incidents that have already occurred. It is a stage or component of emergency management and of risk management. In other words, mitigation either seeks to reduce the likelihood of hazard occurrence or to reduce the negative effects if it were to occur.

Goals of Mitigation: When considering the mitigation options suitable for treating a hazard risk, several general goals classify the outcome that disaster managers may seek.

- **Risk Likelihood Reduction:** Technological and intentional hazards tend to have a greater overall application of measures that seek to reduce hazard likelihood, because the very existence of these hazards is a direct result of human decision. For example, tandem trailers, developed for cargo transport, have been proven to be involved in more accidents than traditional single-trailer rigs. Restricting the use of these vehicles immediately reduces the risk likelihood. While we can't feasibly reduce "decide" not to have a natural hazard, we can do so with other hazard forms. Mitigation measures that seek to reduce risk likelihood tend to be non-structural in nature, though not without exception.
- **Risk Consequences Reduction:** The second primary goal that disaster managers seek to achieve through mitigation is a reduction in the impact of hazard on humans, structures, the environment, or any combination of these. Mitigation measures that address consequences assume that a hazard will occur with an associated intensity or magnitude, and they

ensure that the protected structure, population, system, or other subject is able to withstand such an event without negative consequence. Again using the example of hurricane mitigation, we can see that there is a much greater chance of mitigation success with some hazards when disaster managers address those hazards' consequences. Mechanism enabling structures to be raised above storm surge levels and strengthened against wind damage, storm shelters for affected populations, and regulations restricting actions and activities in high-risk areas all work to considerably reduce the consequences from hurricanes.

Most hazards have one or more options for disaster consequence reduction, which cannot always be said of likelihood reduction. For natural disasters, these measures tend to be structural, and address the hardening of structures and systems and the protection of people. For technological hazards, consequence reduction revolves around the development of primary and redundant safety, containment and clean up systems.

- **Risk Avoidance:** Some hazard risks are so great that even with a partial reduction in either their likelihood or consequence; the resulting outcome is still unacceptable. For these risks only total avoidance is considered, and so it is deemed necessary to take action to reduce either the likelihood or the consequence factor to absolute zero level.

  Total risk avoidance for natural hazards usually means removing all people and structures out of the affected area. Such measures are understandably unrealistic for hazards that have a wide geographic area of impact. Though, Civilizations have tended to avoid such high-risk areas as is evident by the historical lack of development in harsh or dangerous climates such as the Antarctic continent. Risk avoidance may be possible for other types of hazards for which risk is not so all encompassing and can be mapped within regions.

  Risk avoidance is most commonly used in the treatment of technological disasters, for which risk acceptability is subject to more critical consideration in society. In the case of natural disasters, implementing risk avoidance measures in areas that have already been settled can be very difficult, due to socio-cultural and legal matters. Avoidance mitigation often involves uprooting whole communities, at least a temporary reduction in services and quality of life, and the disruption and cultural and social frameworks.

- **Risk Acceptance:** For Certain hazards, disaster managers, as well as societies and individuals, will consider a certain risk to be acceptable "as it is." It may be determined that any further reduction in risk is either too expensive or unnecessary. Several reasons might lead to this decision. First every community, country or region has a range of hazards with which it must contend, and it certainly has a limited pool of funds to deal with that range of hazards. Certain risks, according to their cost-benefit analysis, are not dealt with or left untreated so that funding that would have been consumed by their treatment may be applied to other hazards for which risk reduction will have a greater value.

  Second, some risks reduction measures will result in one or more undesirable consequences. These secondary consequences may simply be the reduction in an enjoyed benefit that exists because of the hazard, or undesirable consequences may be expected to arise as a direct result of the mitigation measure.

  Third, reason for risk acceptance is related to socio-cultural patterns. Many cultures are deeply associated with a certain place or location and would rather face a certain risk than leave for some safer option. Certain religious beliefs make people to think of some risks as divine will, will of some higher power that is beyond their control; therefore they perceive these risks as completely unavoidable.

- **Risk Transfer, Sharing, or Spreading:** The most common forms of risk transfer are insurance coverage and international reinsurance. Insurance reduces the financial consequences of a hazard risk by eliminating the monetary loss of property. Insurers charge a calculated premium, priced according to hazards expected frequency and consequence, which guarantees the repayment of losses, suffered in the event insured against. The cost of disaster is therefore shared by (or "spread across") all customers through the payment premiums. Victims and non-victims alike pay the same premium, for the common fund collected bearing the brunt of the disaster.

Risk sharing, spreading, and insurance schemes appeared as early as 1950 BC when shipping companies began practicing bottomry, the sharing of costs related to maritime risk among all vessels in a fleet.

Q11. What are the various types of mitigation?

Or

Elaborate structural and non-structural mitigation.

Ans. A mitigation action is a specific action, project, activity, or process taken to reduce or eliminate long-term risk to people and property from hazards and their impacts. Implementing mitigation actions helps achieve the plan's mission and goals. The actions to reduce vulnerability to threats and hazards form the core of the plan and are a key outcome of the planning process. The mitigation measures that are employed to achieve the first two goals of mitigation process, a reduction in the likelihood or acceptance of hazard, are grouped into two primary categories: structural and non-structural.

(1) Structural Mitigation: Structural Mitigation is the physical changes or act of protection from disasters or hazards. Structural mitigation measures are those that involve or dictate a necessity for some kind of construction, engineering, or other mechanical changes or improvements aimed at reducing hazard risk likelihood or consequence. They often are considered at "man controlling nature" when applied to natural disasters. Structural measures are generally expensive and include a full range of regulation, compliance, enforcement, inspection, maintenance, and renewal issues.

Though, each hazard a unique set of structural mitigation measures that may be applied to its risk, these measures can be grouped across some general categories.

The general structural mitigation groups to be described are:

- **Resistance Construction:** Clearly the best way to maximize a chance that a structure is able to resist the forces inflicted by various hazards is to ensure that it is designed in such a way prior to construction to do just that. Through awareness and education, individual, corporate, and government entities can be informed of the hazards that exist and the measures that can be taken to mitigate the risks of those hazards, allowing resistant construction to be considered. As a mitigation option, designing hazard resistance into the structure from the start is the most cost-effective option and the option most likely to succeed.

Of course, whether builders choose to use hazard resistant designs depend upon whether they have access to the financial resources, the technical expertise necessary to correctly engineer the construction and the material resources required for such measures.

Where cultures have adapted to living with a hazard, construction styles may incorporate hazard resistant design. This is often seen in areas with annual flooding, where houses are built on stilts. An example of a culturally adjusted hazard resistant construction style is the houses build by the Banni in India, which resist the shaking induced by earthquakes.

- **Building Codes and Resistance measures:** Hazard resistant construction is clearly an effective way to reduce vulnerability to select hazards. However, the builder of the house must apply these resistant construction measures for there to be actual reduction in the population's overall vulnerability. One way that governments can ensure members of the population apply hazard-resistant construction is by creating building codes to guide construction and passing legislation that requires those codes be followed.

  Regulatory structures are one of the most widely adopted structural mitigation measures, used in almost every country of the world in some form. With sufficient knowledge about the hazards likely to affect a region or a country, engineers can develop building codes that guide builders to ensure that their designs are able to resist the forces of the relevant hazards. Though simple in theory, inherent problems with codes and regulation can drastically reduce the effectiveness.

When properly applied building codes offer a great deal of protection from a wide range of hazards. They are primary reason for a drastic drop in the number of earthquake deaths in the developing world during the last century. They are so effective because they completely integrate protective measures into the structure from the design phase onward, rather than applying the measures after construction.

- **Relocation:** Occasionally, the most sensible way to protect a structure or a people from a hazard is to relocate it or them away from the hazard. Homes and other structures may be disassemble or transported intact.

  Flooding is the most common reason that structures are relocated. Though destroying the original structure and rebuilding it elsewhere is often less expensive and technically more feasible, in certain circumstances such actions are either impossible or undesirable. For example the structure in question may be a cultural heritage site that cannot be replaced.

  In some instances where the hazard area is especially great, moving entire communities may be necessary. One such example is the town of Valdez, Alaska, which was relocated in 1967, after hazard assessments showed that the entire town was built upon unstable soil.

- **Structural Modification:** Scientific progress and ongoing research continually provide new information about hazards. This new information can reveal that structures in indentified risk zones are not designed to resist the forces the likely hazard. There are three treatment options for these structures. First is to do nothing. Second the structure may be demolished and rebuilt to accommodate the new hazard information. Third, often the most appropriate action is to modify the structure such that it resists the anticipated external forces. This action is often referred to as retrofitting.

How the retrofit effects the structure depends on the hazard risk that is being dealt with. Some Examples of hazards and their retrofits are:

- **Cyclonic Storms:** Wind resistant shingles; shutters; waterproofing; stronger from connections and joints; structural elevation.
- **Earthquakes:** Sheer Walls; removal of cripple walls; foundation anchor bolts; frame anchor connections; floor framing; chimney reinforcement; base isolation system etc.
- **Wildfire:** Replacement of external materials including decks, gutters, downspouts, paneling doors, window frames and roof shingles, with those that are fire resistant.
- **Hail:** Increase roof slope; strengthen roof materials; strengthen load carrying capacity of flat and shallow angle roofs.

Construction of Community Shelters: The lives of community residents can be protected from a disaster's consequences though the construction of shelters designed to withstand a certain type or range of hazard consequences. Shelters are usually constructed when it is either unlikely or unrealistic for all or a majority of community members to be able to protect themselves from the hazard in their homes or elsewhere. Two systems must be in place in order for shelter to work. First, there must be an effective early warning system that would enable residents to have enough time to travel to the shelter before the hazard event. This immediately rules out several hazards for which warning is impossible or unlikely, such as earthquakes or landslides. Second, there must be a public education campaign that both raises awareness of the existence of the shelter and teacher residents how to recognize when travel to the shelter.

During the Cold War, many countries built shelters or designed qualified buildings to protect citizens from the dangerous fallout effects of a nuclear attack. Shelters are much more likely to be unitized in poor communities throughout the world, where housing construction is especially deficient. For this reason, it is common for community development projects to design community buildings like schools that double as a shelter in the event of a disaster.

Construction of Barrier, Deflection, or Retention Systems: The forces that many hazard exert upon man and the built environment can be controlled through specially engineered structures. These structures fall under three main categories: barriers, deflection system, and retention systems.

Barriers are designed to stop a physical force dead and its tracks. Their job is to absorb the impact of whatever force is being exerted. They are, in other words, blocking devices. Barrier walls can be made of natural materials, such as trees, bushes, or ever existing soil or they can be constructed of foreign materials, such as stone, concrete, wood, or metal. Depending upon the hazard type, barriers may be built on just on side of structure, or may completely surround it. Examples of barriers and the hazards they are designed to protect against include:

- Seawalls (cyclonic storm surges, tsunamis, high waves rough seas, and coastal erosion)
- Floodwalls (Floods, flash floods)
- Natural or synthetic wind and particle movement barriers (strong seasonal winds, sand drift, dune movement, beach erosion, snow drift)
- Defensible spaces (wildfires, forest fires)
- Mass movement protection walls (landslides, mudslides, rockslides, avalanches).
- Security fences, checkpoints (terrorism civil disturbances)

Deflection systems are designed to divert the physical forces of a hazard, allowing it to change course so that a structure situated in its original path escapes harm. Like barriers, deflection systems may be constructed from a full range of materials, both natural and manmade. Examples of deflection systems and the hazards they are designed to protect against include:

- Avalanche bride (snow avalanches)
- Chutes (landslides, mudflows, lahars, rockslides)
- Lava flow channels (volcanic lava)
- Diversion trenches, Channels, canals, and spillway (flood)

Retention systems are designed to contain a hazard, thereby preventing its destructive forces from ever being released. These structure generally seek to increase the threshold to which hazards are physically maintained. Examples include:

- Dams (drought floods)
- Levees and Flood walls (Floods)
- Slit dams (sedimentation, floods)

- Landslide walls (masonry, concrete, rock cage, crib walls, bin walls, and buttress walls)
- Slope stabilisation covers (concrete, netting, wire mesh vegetation landslides mudflows, and rockfalls).

Detection systems are designed to recognize a hazard that might not otherwise be perceptible to humans. They have applications for natural, technological, and international hazards. As more funding is dedicated to research and development of detection systems, their ability to prevent disasters or warn of hazard consequences before disaster strikes increase. With natural disasters, detection systems are primarily used to save lives. With technological and international hazards, however, it may be possible to prevent an attack, explosion, fire, accident, or other damaging event. Examples of detection systems are:

- Imagine satellites (Wildfires, hurricanes, volcanoes, landslides avalanches, floods, fire risk, terrorism, virtually all hazards)
- Chemical/biological/radiological/explosive detection systems (technological hazards (chemical leaks, pipeline failures), terrorism)
- Ground movement monitoring system (seismicity, volcanic activity, dam failure, expansive soils, land subsidence, rail infrastructure failure).
- Flood gauges (hydrologic hazards)
- Weather stations (severe weather, tornadoes)
- Undersea and buoy oceanic movement detection (tsunamis)
- Information system (epidemics, WMD terrorism)

Physical modification is the group of mitigation measures that alters the physical landscape in such a manner that hazard likelihood or consequence is reduced. This can be performed through simple landscaping measures or through the use of engineered devices. Ground modification examples include:

- Slope terracing-landslides, mudflows, erosion.
- Slope drainage-landslides, mudflows, erosion.
- Regarding of steep slopes-landslides, mudflows, rockfalls, erosion, avalanches
- Anchors and piling-landslides

- Removal and/or replacement of soil-expansive soils
- Wetland reclamation-flooding
- Dredging rivers-flooding
- Dredging reservoirs-drought

Treatment systems seek to remove a hazard from a natural system that humans depend on. These systems may be designed for non-stop use or for use in certain circumstances where a hazard is known to be present. Examples include:

- Water treatment systems
- HEPA air filtration ventilation systems
- Airborne pathogen decontamination system
- Hazardous materials (HAZMAT) decontamination systems.

Redundancy in life Safety infrastructure is one last structural mitigation measure. As humans hand evolved beyond substance living. they have become more dependent upon each other and societal infrastructure. Today, private and government infrastructure may provide and individual with food, water sewerage, electricity, communications, transportation medical care, and more, With such great dependence on these systems, failure in any one could quickly lead in catastrophe. Example of life systems into which redundancy may be built include:

- Electricity infrastructure
- Public Health Infrastructure
- Emergency management infrastructure
- Water storage, treatment, conveyance, and delivery systems
- Transportation infrastructure
- Irrigation systems
- Food delivery

(2) Non-structural mitigation: Non-structural mitigation in emergency management involves what people can do on a personal level that is not structurally or physically evident as a protective defense such as a surge wall or a storm shelter. Non- structural mitigation in general would involve things such as having flood insurance.

Non-structural Mitigation generally involves a reduction in the likelihood or consequence of risk through modifications in human behavior or natural processes, without requiring the use of engineered structures. Non-structural mitigation techniques are often considered mechanisms where man adapts to nature. They tend to be less costly and fairly easy for communities with few financial or technological resources to implement.

The following are various categories into which non-structural mitigation measures may be grouped, and provides several examples or each:

Regulatory Measure: Regulatory measures limit hazard risk by legally dictating human actions. Regulations can be applied to several facets of societal and individual life, and are when it is determined that such action is required for the common good of the society. Though the use of regulatory measures is perspective, compliance is a widespread problem because the cost of enforcement can be prohibitive and inspectors may be untrained, ineffective, or susceptible to bribes.

Examples or regulatory mitigation measures include:

- Land use management (Zoning). This legally imposed restriction on now land may be used. It may apply to specific geographic designation, such as coastal Zone management hillside or slope management, floodplain development restriction, or microclimate siting of structures (such as placing structures only he leeward side of a hill)
- Open space preservation (green spaces). This practice attempts to limit the settlement or activities of people in areas that are known to be at high risk for one more hazards.
- Protective resource preservation. In some situations, a tract of land is not at risk from a hazard, but a new hazard will be created by disturbing that land. Examples include protecting forest that serves to block wind and wetlands preservation.
- Denial of services to high-risk areas. When squatter and informal settlements from on high risk land despite the existence of preventive regulatory measures, it is possible to discourage growth and reverse settlement trends by ensuring that services such as electricity running water, and communications do not reach the unsafe settlement. This measure is not only acceptable when performed in conjunction with a project that seeks to offer alternative, safe

accommodations for the inhabitants (otherwise, a secondary humanitarian disaster may result)

- Density control. By regulatory the number of people who may reside in an area of known or estimated risk, it is possible to limit vulnerability and control the amount of resources considered adequate for protection from and response to that known hazard. Many response mechanisms are overwhelmed because the number of casualties in an affected area is much higher than was anticipated.
- Building use regulations: To protect against certain hazards, it is possible to restrict the type of activities that may be performed in a building. These restrictions may apply to people, materials, or activates.
- Mitigation easements. Easements are agreements between private individuals or organisations and the government that dictate now a particular tract of land will be used. Mitigation easements are agreements to restrict the private use of land for the purpose of risk reduction.
- HAZMAT manufacture, use, transport, and disposal. Hazardous materials are a major threat to life and property in all countries. Most governments have developed safety standards and procedures to guide the way that these materials are manufactured and used by businesses and individuals, the mechanisms by which they are transported from place to place, and the methods and devices that contain them.
- Safety standards and regulations. Regulations that guide safe activities and practices are diverse and apply to more situations that could be described in this chapter. Safety regulations may apply to individual (seatbelt laws), households (use of smoke detectors), communities, business, and governments. The establishment of building codes, as described in the section on structure mitigation, is an example of a safely regulation.
- Natural resource use regulations. The use of common natural resources, such as aquifers, can be controlled for the purpose of minimizing hazard risk (in this case, drought).

- Storm water management regulations. Storm water run-off can be destructive to the areas where run-off can be destructive to the areas where it originates, through erosion, and to the areas where it terminates, through silting, pollution, changes to stream flows, and other effects. Development, especially when large amount of land are covered with impervious materials like concrete, can drastically increase the amount of run-off by decreasing the holding capacity of the land.
- Environmental Protection regulations. Certainly environmental features, such as rivers, stream lakes, and wetlands, play an important part of reducing the vulnerability of community of country. Preventing certain behaviors, such as dumping of polluting helps to ensure that the resources continue to offer their risk reduction benefits.
- Public disclosure regulations. Property owned may be required to disclose all known risk, so as flood or earthquake hazard risk, when selling their property. This ensures hazard awareness and increases the chance that purchasers will take appropriate action for those known risk when they begin construction or other activities on that land.
- Mitigation requirements on loans. Banks and other lending institutions have much at stake when they lend money to developers. Therefore lenders should ensure that mitigation requirements should be met, which require that hazard assessments have been conducted. Governments can make it a policy that such actions are taken by those leading institutions. Such policies limit the building of unsafe projects.

Community Awareness and Education Programs: The public is most able to protect themselves from the effects of a hazard if they are first informed that the hazard exists, and then educated about what they can do to limit their risk.

- Public education programs are considered both mitigation and preparedness measures. An informed public that applied appropriate measures to reduce their risk before a disaster occurs has performed mitigation. However, a public that has been trained in response activities has participated in a preparedness activity. Often termed "risk communication," projects designed to educate the public may include one or more of the following: (i) Awareness of the hazard risk (ii) Behavior (iii) Pre-disaster risk reduction behavior (iv) Pre-disaster preparedness behavior (v) Post-disaster response behavior (vi) Post-disaster recovery behavior

- Warning systems inform the public that hazard risk which has reached a threshold required certain protective actions. Depending upon the hazard type and the warning system's technological capabilities, the amount of time citizens will have to act will vary. Some warning systems, especially those that apply to technological and international hazards, are not able to provide warning until the hazard has already begun to exhibit its damaging behavior (such as a leak at a chemical production facility, or an accident involving a hazardous materials tanker truck). The UN Platform for the Promotion of early warning (PPEW) state that four separate factors are necessary for effective early warning. (1) Prior knowledge of the risks faced by communities. (2) A technical monitoring and warning services for these risks. (3) The dissemination of understandable warnings to those at risk. (4) Knowledge by people of how to react and the capacity to do go.

Warning systems, therefore, are dependent upon hazard identification and analyze, effective detection systems (as described in Structural Mitigation), and public education. Early warning system have been developed to varying capacities for the following hazards:

— Drought

— Tornados

— Cyclonic storms

— Epidemics

— Landslides

— Earthquakes

— Chemical release

— Volcanoes

— Floods

— Wildfires

— Air raids/attacks

— Terrorist theats

Risk mapping involves presenting the likelihood and consequence components in the format of a physical map, with figures based upon a specific hazard of set of hazards. Risk maps are fundamental to disaster management, and are very effective as a mitigation tool. Using risk maps, governments and other entities can most effectively dedicate resources to areas of greatest need, and plan in advance of incidents, so that adequate response resources are able to reach those highest-risk areas without unforeseen problems.

Non-structural Physical Modifications: Several different mitigation option, while not structure in nature, involve a physical modification to a structure or to property that result in reduced risk.

Examples include

- *Security of furniture, pictures, and appliances, and installing latches on cup boards.* In many earthquakes, the majority of injuries are caused by falling furniture and other unsecured belongings. Economic coasts also can be reduced significantly through this very inexpensive, simple measure that generally requires little more than connecting items to walls through the use of a specially designed then metal strep.
- *Removal or securing of projectiles.* During tornadoes, items commodity found outside the house, such as cooking grills, furniture, and stored wood, may become airborne projectiles than cause harm, fatalities, or further property damage.

Environmental Control: Structural mitigation involves engineered structures that control hazards. It is also possible to control or influence hazards through non-engineered structural means. These non-structural mechanisms tend to be highly hazard specific, and include:

- Explosive detonation to relieve seismic pressure (earthquakes)
- Launched or placed explosive to release stored snow cover (avalanches)
- Cloud seeding (hail, hurricanes, drought, and snow)
- Controlled burns (wildfires)
- Bombing of Volcano flows

- Dune and beach restoration or preservation (storm surges, erosion)
- Forest and vegetation management (landslide mudflow, flooding, erosion)
- Riverine and reservoir sediment and erosion control (flooding)
- Replacement of soils (expansive soils)
- Hillside drainage (landslides, mudslide erosion)
- Slope grading (landslides, mudslides, rockfalls erosion)
- Disease vector eradication (Epidemics)

Behavior Modification: Through collective action, a community can alter the behavior of individual; resulting in some common risk reduction benefit. Voluntary behavior modification measures are more difficult to implement than the regulatory measures listed above. Because they usually involve some form of sacrifice. However, through effective public education behavior modification is possible. Tax incentives, or subsides, can help to increase the success of behavioral modification practices Examples of mitigation measures that involve behavior modification include:

- Rationing: Rationing is often performed prior to and during period of drought. Because it can be very difficult for governments to limit vital services such as water to citizens, it is up to citizenships to limit their individual usage. Electricity rationings is also performed during periods of extreme heat or cold to ensure that electrical control systems are able to perform as required.
- Environmental conservation: Many practices to both urban and rural areas are very destructive to the environment. Once the environmental feature be it a body of water, a forest, of the hillside is destroyed, secondary hazards consequences may appear that could have avoided. Though proper education and the offering of alternative, destructive practices can be halted before too much damage is done. Examples of environmental conservation include and ornamentally friendly farming practices and harvesting that does not cause deforestation and protecting coral reefs from dynamite fishing and other fishing practices.

- Tax incentives, subsidies, and other financial rewards for safe practices: Individuals and businesses can be coaxed into safer practices that reduce overall risk through financial incentive.

  Examples of schemes that use financial initiative include lower insurance premiums, housing buyout programs to move out of high-risk area and farm subsidies for allowing land to be used for flood control during emergencies, and environmentally friendly farming practices (no deforestation, responsible grazing practices, flexible framing and cropping).
- *Strengthening of social ties:* When a community strengthens its social ties, it is more likely to withstand a hazard's stresses. For many reasons the largest of which is urbanisation, these ties break and are not replaced. In Chicago in 1995 a heat wave caused the death of 739 people. It was later determined that weak social structures which have been prevented friends, family a neighbours checked on the victims.

Q12. Define the meaning of gender and sex. Differentiate between both of them.

Or

What is the difference between gender and sex?

Ans. Gender: Gender is the range of characteristics pertaining to, and differentiating between, masculinity and femininity. Depending on the context, these characteristics may include biological sex (i.e., the state of being male, female, or an intersex variation), sex-based social structures (i.e., gender roles), or gender identity. Traditionally, people who identify as men or women or use masculine or feminine gender pronouns are using a system of gender binary whereas those who exist outside these groups fall under the umbrella terms non-binary or gender queer. Some cultures have specific gender roles that are distinct from "man" and "woman," such as the hijras of South Asia. These are often referred to as third genders.

Sex: Organisms of many species are specialized into male and female varieties, each known as a sex. Sexual reproduction involves the combining and mixing of genetic traits: specialized cells known as gametes combine to form offspring that inherit traits from each parent. The gametes produced by an organism define its sex: males produce small gametes (e.g. spermatozoa, or sperm, in animals; pollen in seed plants) while females produce large gametes (ova, or egg cells). Individual organisms which produce both male and female gametes are termed hermaphroditic. Gametes can be identical in form and function (known as isogamy), but, in many cases, an asymmetry has evolved such that two different types of gametes (heterogametes) exist (known as anisogamy).

Distinction between sex and gender: The distinction between sex and gender differentiates a person's biological sex (the anatomy of an individual's reproductive system, and secondary sex characteristics) from that person's gender, which can refer to either social roles based on the sex of the person (gender role) or personal identification of one's own gender based on an internal awareness (gender identity). In this model, the idea of a "biological gender" is an oxymoron: the biological aspects are not gender-related, and the gender-related aspects are not biological. In some circumstances, an individual's assigned sex and gender do not align, and the person may be transgender. In other cases, an individual may have biological sex characteristics that complicate sex assignment, and the person may be intersex.

The sex and gender distinction is not universal. In ordinary speech, sex and gender are often used interchangeably. Some dictionaries and academic disciplines give them different definitions while others do not. Some languages, such as German or Finnish, have no separate words for sex and gender, and the distinction has to be made through context. On occasion, using the English word gender is appropriate.

Among scientists, the term sex differences (as compared to gender differences) is typically applied to sexually dimorphictraits that are hypothesized to be evolved consequences of sexual selection.

Gender	**Sex**
Social construction	Biological construction
Differential in nature	Universal in nature
Connotes different social roles of men and women in society. e.g. male as breadwinners, women performing household chores	Connotes only physical difference e.g. the way we are biologically born

Q13. Elucidate the vulnerability of women and men in disasters.

Ans. Women are generally considered to be more vulnerable during disasters. The reasons for their vulnerability can be categorized into four major categories which are as follows:

- **Biologically** speaking women tend to have lesser physical strength as compared to men. In the recent tsunami, in Cuddalore, almost three times, as many women as men, were killed, with 391 female deaths, compared with 146 men. The women could not run as fast as men could to save themselves not only on account of their physical strength but their cultural attire of sari also prohibited them from running along with their children. The sheer strength to stay alive in the torrent was also decisive in deciding the survivors. Many women and young children, unable to stay on their feet, or afloat, in the wave, simply tired and drowned Women clinging to one or more children would tend to tire even more quickly. Moreover the biological vulnerability of women is enhanced during disasters as they have to face certain reproductive health problems which are highly specific to their sex. The plight of menstruating women or pregnant women who have to deliver or survive in a situation where all construction has collapsed and everyone is out in the open is unfathomable.
- **Economically,** women are generally considered to be poorer than men on account of their lower incomes, lack of job stability, dependence on the income of men, scant recognition of their productive labour and limited access to resources with potential to produce income, Socio-cultural beliefs and practices often-preclude women's ownership of land and other production technologies such as tractors or grinding mills. Lack of credit facilities, knowledge of how to access credit, and marketing and bargaining skills commonly affect women. They have lesser access to resources like transportation, skills and information. They are also victims of gendered division of labour as majority of them in India are working in underpaid and unrepresented jobs with no union representation.
- **Sociologically,** women have enjoyed an adjunct status to men in the patriarchal Indian society. In many parts of the country,

women face a culture devaluation from the members. The heinous practices of female infanticide and female foeticide uphold this devaluation. A study reported that out of five million girls born every year; one fourth of them did not live to see their fifteenth birthday. Despite being genetically stronger, three lakh more girls died in India than boys every year. More distressing was the fact that one in every six female deaths was due to gender discrimination.

The patriarchal society coupled with specific gender connotations in India make them victims do domestic violence, subjects them to the incessant toil of performing household chores within the four walls of the house, restricts their mobility, and marginalizes them in most of the decisions taken by the family. The social connotation of an adjunct status to men marginalizes the needs of women in emergencies.

- **Psychologically,** the mental makeup of woman makes her a more sensitive and emotional being who faces greater stress as compared to a man in her everyday life. She experiences greater stress due to her multiple responsibilities and generally inferior social status. It decreases her resistance to diseases and adversely affects her ability to undertake essential economic and family activities. As far as India is concerned, after the Gujarat Riots, a study was conducted in one of the affected villages of Anand Khera on the mental health of the patients. It was found that women, children and the elderly reported more symptoms which were suggestive of depression in the aftermath of the human induced disaster. The vulnerability of men in disasters stems from their social and economic roles ascribed to them. Social factors play their role and society sees them as 'bread earners of the family'. Men are expected to bear the full financial responsibility for their families. They do not know how to perform household chores and face problems incase they have to perform household chores and take care of children. Men tend to bear the responsibility of protecting of their families which cannot be fulfilled in the wake of a disaster.

Psychologically, men are generally socialized not to express their emotions. They tend to suppress their emotions even in times of crisis resulting in stress and trauma.

Q14. What are the different impacts of disasters on men and women?

Or

What are the various effects of disasters on men and women?

Ans. Disaster affects men and women in a different manner. Women are considered to bear the brunt of disasters more severely, as compared to men on account of their gender. Some of the gender issues in the management of disasters in the pre and post-disasters phase are described below. The issues are supported and illustrated by studies conducted in the field of disaster management by varied practitioners and researchers.

Early Warning: Gender is an important factor in the dissemination of early warning issued during an emergency.

In the ensuing procrastination, women who had comparatively less knowledge about cyclones and were dependent on male decision-making, perished, many with their children, waiting for their husbands to return home and take them to safety.

Evacuation: Effective and timely response to early warning calls for an immediate decision of evacuation of the community from the vulnerable area. Evacuation is an important decision, taken in the golden hours of an impending a disaster, which can single handedly determine the mortality and morbidity rate of the vulnerable population. The vulnerability of women is accentuated during this critical phase as they are constrained by cultural norms that restrict women's freedom of movement in public. Many women waited for their husbands to return home to take the decision to evacuate, thereby losing precious time that might have saved their lives and those of their children. The status of women in society generally determines the process of decision making for evacuation. In many developing countries decision making is generally in the hands of men and thus the decision to evacuates is primarily seen as the domain of men.

Search and Rescue: Gender variation in mortality and morbidity vary by disaster type and location in the disaster. In 1994, twice as many males died in weather related hazards, such as winter storms, thunderstorms and lightening. These hazards affected males as they were the ones who participated in work and leisure activities and most of these deaths occurred outside home, in vehicles and in the open. However, more females died in the Indian Ocean tsunami as women remained home while men were fishing on the sea; during the Latur earthquake in Maharashtra in 1993, fewer men than women died because they happened to be sleeping outdoors because of the worm weather. Moreover, because the gender division of labour kept women in or closer to homes, it was generally women who suffered disproportionately from the collapse of poorly constructed dwellings.

Medical Aid: In many tradition societies women would not go to a male doctor for first aid or treatment. Provision of medical aid and ensuring their accessibility to the affected women are critical areas of concern in emergency management in such societies. Soon after the Pakistan earthquake in October, 2005 newspapers highlighted stories about the need of female doctors in providing medical aid to the women disaster survivors after the devastating earthquake as families were very hesitant to bring the doctors to the tents or to take the women to the medical units as doctors were mostly men. Women in a culture such as Pakistan are not used to talking with strangers, and this has caused many hurdles in getting them needed help, medical and other wise. They feel shy to come forward with their problems, and medical aid givers have had to make special efforts to reach women.

Shelter: Temporary shelters are put into place and survivors are forced to live in congested relief camps, but through these processes the needs of privacy and care for the more vulnerable group of pregnant, lactating and menstruating women are not adequately taken care of. Availability of space for all the members of the family plays a crucial role in determining whether the need for shelter has been fulfilled with a gender sensitivity approach. It is also necessary that the gender division of labour within households before, during and after the disaster is understood and reflected in the location, design and layout of shelters. In the aftermath of 1991 cyclone in Bangladesh, women who are able to reach the temporary shelters found them ill suited to meet gender and culture specific needs; in a social context where seclusion is practiced, larger number of men and women were crowded in together with no respect to privacy for pregnant, lactating and menstruating women.

Similarly in the layout and design of intermediary and permanent shelters the specific needs of women and girls are often not taken care of.

Physical and Mental Health: Studies have reported adverse reproductive health problems following a disaster, including early pregnancy loss, premature delivery, stillbirths, delivery related complications and infertility. There are various health related issues pertinent to women after a disaster on account of their reproductive responsibility. Firstly, the pregnant and lactating women need pre-natal and post natal care in the aftermath of a disaster. Secondly, social taboos around menstruation and norms about appropriate behavior for women and girls are reported to contribute to health problems in disaster situations. During the 1998 floods in Bangladesh, adolescent girls reported perennial rashes and urinary tract infections because they were not able to wash out menstrual rags properly in private and often had no place to hang the rags to dry, or access clean water. They reported wearing the damp cloths, as they did not have place to dry them.

Gender-Based Violence: A disaster event is not a sufficient condition to initiate gender based violence against women. Rather, an individual's place within the social structure influences the likelihood of him/her becoming a disaster victim or of experiencing conditions that may worsen their vulnerability.

During a natural disaster or a crisis, institutions and systems for physical and social protection may be weakened or destroyed. Police, legal, health, education and social services are often disrupted; many people flee, and those who remain may not have the capacity or the equipment to work. Families and communities are often separated, which results in a further breakdown of community support systems and protection mechanisms.

Violence is also exacerbated by the disruption of support and protection mechanisms. Literature specifically focusing on this issue is extremely scarce and the only widely available detailed research is by one author, Elaine Enarson.

Relief Management: Relief mechanisms, as are currently practiced, need to look into the specific needs of women. Moreover, traditionally female participation in disaster management has largely been related to the role of caring and nurturing. There is limited representation of women on national and local emergency committees and their potential as a resource for organized action at all levels of the managerial process has been seriously overlooked. Therefore, an effective relief management strategy has to be built upon two pillars namely; addressing the specific needs of women and ensuring their participation and involvement in the management process.

Q15. Discuss the process of mainstreaming of gender in disaster management.

Ans. The process of mainstreaming varied gender issues in disaster management need to be done at the planning level in pre-disaster times. Both men and women need to be involved in all phases to ensure that the specific needs of each gender are met and a gender sensitive approach is adopted during emergencies. The following Table highlights the ways to mainstream gender in generating early warning of disasters to men and women.

S. No.	Early Warning Function	Tool
1.	Dissemination	• Use both formal and informal means of warning dissemination. • Ensure that warnings are issued at every doorstep of the vulnerable population rather than limiting to public places only. • Involve both men and women as agents of warning dissemination.
2	Awareness	• Explain the meaning of the warning to women as they may not have the necessary information to understand the warning signals. • Generate awareness through the formal and informal means targeting women to identify the danger signals and evacuate. • Highlight the importance of early warning and the need to adhere to the warning issued.

Evacuation and Search and Rescue operations are a vital phase for determining the mortality rate for men and women in disaster. Table 2 and Table show ways to mainstream gender during these phases so that men and women get an equal chance of survival.

Table : Gender and Evacuation

S. No.	Evacuation Function	Tool
1	Information	• Disseminate information about the safe escape route to the entire community including the more vulnerable group. • Include both men and women in dissemination of information and ensure that such information reaches women. • Conduct periodic mock drill in high disaster prone areas. • Appoint and nodal officer who would coordinate the evacuation of women and children.
2	Transportation	• Provide transportation facilities for evacuation of women and children especially for pregnant and lactating mothers.
3	Training and sensitization	• Train the team assisting in evacuation of the vulnerable community to deal with women who would not evacuate on account of the prevalent socio-cultural practices. • Sensitize the women to make immediate decisions of timely evacuation on their own as it would help in saving lives.

Table : Gender and Search and Rescue (SAR) Operations

S. No.	SAR Function	Tool
1	Composition of the Response force.	• Ensure that the SAR team includes members of both sexes.
2	Mapping	• Conduct needs analysis of men and women before initiating a rescue operation. • Prepare checklist of differential needs of men and women prepared.
3	Social Inhibitions/Cultural practices	• Response force is trained in dealing with women rendered immobile by social practices like purdah system and unwillingness to touch another man.
4	Special Vulnerability	• SAR team is trained and fully

		equipped to rescue and provide first aid to pregnant women. • SAR team is trained in rescuing physically and mentally challenged women. • One member is trained and well versed with sign language

Provision of timely medical aid is important for saving lives of men and women. The medical aid services are generally operated by men. These services inevitably land up being used by mean as women feel shy and embarrassed to approach men for help and assistance. Hence the provision and accessibility of medical aid services need to be designed meticulously for cutting across the gender barriers in a post disaster scenario. Table shows the tools and techniques that should be used to mainstream gender in medical aid function.

Table : Gender and Medical Aid

S. No.	Medical Aid Function	Tool
1	Medical Services	• Recruit female staff wherever possible. • Set up a private consultation/examination room for women and girls. • Female obstetricians and gynecologists should be included in medical teams servicing camps and affected communities. • Ensure that women do not hesitate or feel shy or fearful in consulting the medical team on problems.
2	Accessibility of Services	• Locate health services within walking distance of communities and on safe access roads. • Clinics should be located in close proximity to the relief camp. • Make opening times of the clinics convenient for women and children keeping in view their involvement in household duties.

Provision of shelter with respect of adequet design, layout, space and location is vital to ensure that the gender needs of both women and men are met after a disaster. Table 5 shows important gendered functions of shelter management and tools to fulfill those functions.

Table : Gender and Shelter

S. No.	Shelter Function	Tool
1	Design and Layout	• Consult men and women in the design and layout of camps and shelters focusing on women as they are the prime users and managers of the shelter. • Mobilize women and men to participate in the location, design, and maintenance of water and sanitation facilities. • Prepare an activity clock which will give a fair idea about the specific needs of women and men that need to be accommodated. Discussion with women on the way activities are carried out and their suitable space allocations can lead to useful inputs for shelter design. • Make every possible effort to relocate widows, adolescent girls, and physically and mentally challenged women in temporary shelters which are centrally located. • Take the inputs of women which can help design spaces suitable for children. • Temporary shelters should be built close to schools and hospitals. • Ensure that the shelter has a minimum of $45m^2$ surface area of camp per person including infrastructure except in extreme circumstances.
2	Space and Location	• Shelter should be in close proximity to fuel collection and other activities that involve movement outside the designated sites. • Provide a common area for children to play where family members can watch them from the shelter, to avoid children playing in remote areas. • Make adequate arrangements for lighting in temporary shelters particularly in common facilities like toilets, bathrooms etc. • Provide adequate material for partitions between families in a temporary shelter.

The reproductive health of disaster survivors, especially women is one of the most important aspect that has to be looked into in a post-disaster scenario. The specific needs of pregnant and lactating mothers have to understood and fulfilled timely and adequately. Vital issues like menstruation, contraception and recannilisation also have to dealt with sensitivity to ensure a gender sensitive approach to disaster management. Table indicates the tools that can be used to carry out the reproductive health functions.

Table : Gender and Reproductive Health

S. No.	Reproductive Health Function	Tool
1	Pregnant and Lactating women	• Identify a qualified and experienced person to coordinate maternal health activities at the start of an Emergency response within each camp/area and within each implementing agency. • Sensitize the family and others in the relief camp to understand the special needs of the pregnant women, women who have aborted and needs of the women who have delivered. • Identify health workers with midwifery skills and other health workers amongst survivors to provide care for childbirth. • Identify women who are in advanced stages of pregnancy and where to deliver, how to recognize danger signs and where to seek help. • Give each pregnant woman a delivery kit. • Half a day sensitization of disaster survivors in each camp on danger signs, usage of delivery kit location of immediate hospital, referral facilities and care for women who have had abortion during the disaster. • Provide 24-hour access for complications of pregnancy services. • The lactating mothers who have lost their children be given medical aid to prevent clotting in their breasts. • Gear up hospitals to deal with increase in the number of cases of abortions, stillbirths and early delivery.
2	Menstruation	• Distribute sanitary packs at regular intervals throughout the emergency and distribute to any new arrivals. • In some situations, the first distribution of sanitary materials will need to occur without community consultations, in order to avoid delay. Subsequently, consult with women and girls to identify materials most culturally appropriate.

		• Equip the temporary toilets with incinerator for proper disposal of sanitary material. • In case sanitary cloths are being used, mark out a private laundering area in each camp to wash sanitary cloths.
3	Contraception	• Adequate provision and easy access to different forms of contraception be facilitated as soon as possible. • Contraceptive should be a vital component of the relief kit. • Distribute contraceptives only through women.
4	Recannalisation	• Free recannalisation facility should be made accessible and available to a couple. • The couple is given counseling before the surgery is performed focusing on the benefits and risks associated with the recannalisation operative measures for the women. It should be explained that women should not be blamed for unable to get pregnant after recannalisation. • Surgery is performed keeping in view the physical age as well as the mental well being of a woman. • Wider counseling of the community should be done in order to think on broader terms of adopting orphaned kids and accepting them as their own.

The increase in gender based violence is common occurrence after a disaster. Augmentation of liquor consumption by men, breakdown of liquor consumption by men, breakdown of family support systems, disruption of social security measures are some of the reasons for the increased GBV activities after a disaster. The aspect of delivery of services for curbing gender-based violence, making adequate provisions for safety and security for disaster survivors as well as providing counseling for victims of gender-based violence have to be taken care of in a post disaster situation. Table lists out the tools that can be used to mainstream gender in curbing gender based violence after a disaster.

Table : Gender and Gender-Based Violence

S. No.	(GBV) Function	Tool
1	Delivery of Services	• Locate the food and water services in close proximity to the shelters. • Ensure that the services are delivered during daylight and

		the paths well lit during evenings. • Monitor security and instances of abuse in the distribution point as well as on departure roads. • Do not make women and girls dependent on men for shelter construction or shelter allocation because this often results in sexual exploitation, with women forced to trade sex for shelter.
2	Provisions of safety	• Form vigilance committees in each community/camp consisting of men and women to act as monitoring officers. • Develop written and verbal safety guidelines against possible violations against women. • Train women to raise immediate alarms against violations in the camp sites. • Station women police officers to record and address safety complaints made by affected women in the camps and monitor women's rights violation in the camps. • Maintain night security at camps. • Train security guards of both sexes to be sensitive to apprehensions and problems of women in order to facilitate assistance seeking by women. • Seek ongoing inputs from women to ensure that their needs and security concerns are addressed. • Ban the use of alcohol near disaster affected area. • Provide free legal services to survivors of sexual violence.
3	Counseling	• Discuss issues of sexual violence, survivors' needs for emotional support, and evaluate the individuals, groups, and organisations available in the community to ensure they will be supportive, compassionate, non-judgmental, confidential, and respectful towards survivors. • Counsel the affected women by assurance, adopting a non-judgmental approach, empowering the affected woman to cope up with the situation in a positive manner with the help of social support, spiritualism and recreation.

The approach of "one blanket fits all" during the relief phase of disaster management has to be done away with. It has to be understood that men and women have specific needs which have to be fulfilled differently. The constitution of relief supplies and information disseminations in relief camps should be done with a gender sensitive approach. Men and women should be done with a gender sensitive approach. Men and women should both be involved in the planning and operationalisation of relief camp services. Table 8 indicate the tools that can be used to mainstream gender in relief management in a post-disaster scenario.

Table : Gender and Relief Management

S. No.	Relief Function	Tool
1	Relief Camp Management	• Nominate both men and women in camp management teams/committees. • Encourage women in camp decision making. • Ensure that they are not represented by male family members in camp management. • Hold meetings on camp management at convenient times for women members to attend. • Ensure that each camp has a separate enclosure for private needs of pregnant, lactating and menstruation women.
2	Relief Supplies	• Provide clothing for men and women according to their culture and age. • Design the contents of the relief kit in consultation with both men and women. • Make it a point to include undergarments, contraceptives and culturally appropriate sanitary material in the relief kit (already mentioned in the earlier toolkit on health) • Include both men and women in the distribution of relief aid. • Incase undergarments, contraceptives and sanitary material are being distributed in the relief camps, ensure that they are distributed only through women and not through

		men.
3	Information Dissemination	• Appoint male and female officers in each camp to coordinate the dissemination of information on Relief assistance being provided by the government, compensation packages, Ex-Gratia payments etc. • Ensure that the efforts are made to reach out to women in shelters within the camps as in some cultures women do not participate in public meetings where information is being announced.

❑❑❑

Chapter-3

Emergency Response

Q1. Explain major considerations for relief management.

Or

Elucidate relief management in India. What are the essential components of Relief Management?

Ans. Essential Components of Relief Management: In order to ensure that relief commodities and services are made available to the real needy ones at the place and time required, it is essential to follows certain operational guidelines as follows:

- Designate a person (or a group of persons) within the supply section as the focal point(s) for the given disaster.
- Establish a mini emergency supply team for targeted action-oriented implementation, as a means or minimizing disruption of on-going supply functions while meeting emergency needs.
- Coordinate through concerned departments/ministries with other partners and counterparts to streamline supply procurement and avoid duplication.
- Provide suggestions on potential supply sources, as may be helpful to partners.
- Work with the Emergency Task Force (this could be operating under a different nomenclature) to finalize and establish correct products, specifications, quantities, qualities, destinations, distribution and storage systems.

- Assess sources prices and availability to determine local or offshore options.
- Initiate the procurement process, keeping a provision for flexibility in decision-making and operation processes to meet emergency requirements.
- Establish an active communication mechanism that provides up-to-date about all supply activities, ensuring that all key players have access to the latest information.
- For items not available locally, coordinate emergency offshore procurement, including charter flight, port clearance, delivery and redistribution.
- Monitor the procurement, supply and distribution processes.

As a number of stakeholders participate in the process of providing relief it becomes obvious that specific roles and responsibilities need to be assigned to such actors for:

- Assisting the government other national and international agencies in the distribution of relief items;
- Ensuring that interventions are not duplicated and the most vulnerable are reached with relief and rehabilitation measures;
- Ensuring that the people in need receive their entitlements and compensation as appropriate.

Relief Management in India: According to studies, India is world's most disaster prone country. The nation is troubled by various types of natural disasters every year like floods, drought and earthquakes. A large number of people are affected every year and the economic losses caused by natural disasters amount to a major share of the Gross National Product (GNP). These kinds of natural disasters are immense economic burdens on developing economies like India. It is being noted that every year, a great amount of resources are used for rescue and restoration works for disaster.

Disaster management being a State subject in India, at the State level, the State Relief Commissioner or Secretary, directs and controls the relief operations through District Collectors or Deputy Commissioners, who are the king-pins of all relief operations, coordination, direction and control at the District level.

(1) Relief Codes and Manuals: The State Governments have formulated their Relief Manuals (or Codes) and the Districts have their Contingency Plans, which are updated from time to time based on the experience. Routinely, NGOs and community are invited before the monsoon to share the contingency plan. In case of a disaster, the State Government invites NGOs and other relief organizations to join in the efforts in reaching out to the victims.

Majority of the existing State Relief Manuals carry a "scarcity" focus while addressing Relief. However, given the changing' nature of disaster response coupled with the experience gained from recent disasters in the country, now a effort is under way by the Central Government to re-orient the existing State Relief Manuals and Codes with a "mitigation, prevention and preparedness" focus. With variations in details, a typical State Relief Manual in the country usually contains following (or similar) provisions for management of relief:

- The system of Intelligence defining Authorities and Officials
- Programs and Estimates for Various Relief Works
- Reserves of Establishment and Tools
- Preliminary Preparation and Test
- Declaration of Scarcity and Commencement of Relief
- Powers and Duties of Supervising Officers including Police Officers, Medical and Public Health Officers
- The Organization of Village Inspection and Relief
- Organization of Relief Works
- Wages and Allowance on Relief Works
- Gratuitous Relief
- Rains Policy and Closure of Relief, Closure of Scarcity
- Provisions for Cattle and Fodder, Drinking Water
- Procedures for Maintenance of Accounts
- Involvement of Voluntary Agencies
- Tagavi Loans and Subsidies
- Relief for Other Calamities

(2) Calamity Relief Fund (CRF): Relief and rehabilitation measures in the event of natural disasters is that of the concerned State Government. The role of the Central Government is supportive, in term of supplementing physical and financial resources and complementary measures in sectors like warning, transport and inter-State movement of food grains etc. The policy and arrangements for meeting relief expenditure are, by and large, based on the recommendations of the successive Finance Commissions. Earlier, margin money was allocated to each State for meeting the immediate needs of expenditure on relief measures. The quantum of margin money was calculated by averaging the non-plan expenditure (excluding advance plan assistance and expenditure of a plan nature) on relief measures.

The margin money so provided for each of the States was duly taken into account while working out the forecast of expenditure for each of the State, on the basis of which the Finance Commission Finalized its recommendations for the devolution or resources for the period covered by them.

(3) National Fund for Calamity Relief (NFCR): For dealing with calamities of "rare severity" requiring Central intervention, the Tenth Finance Commission suggested creation of National Fund for Calamity Relief. The fund was to be managed by a National Calamity Relief Fund Committee (NCRFC). In the absence of a clear definition of the term "rare severity", the functioning of the NCRC has been haunted by a number of problems due to States asking for Central assistance for all types of calamities.

(4) Provisions under the National Disaster Response Plan: The National Disaster Response Plan prepared by the High Powered Committee in September 2001 has cast the overall responsibility for the provision of relief supplies on the Ministry of Planning and Programme Implementation as the primary agency. This Emergency Support Function lists the following responsibilities for the Primary Agency:

- Coordinate activities involved with the emergency provisions;
- Temporary shelter;
- Emergency mass feeding;
- Bulk distribution;
- To provide logistical and resource support to local entities;
- Operate a Disaster Welfare Information (DWI) System to collect, receive, and report the status of victims, assist family reunification and coordinate bulk distribution of emergency relief supplies; and

- In some instance, services also may be provided to disaster workers.

Relief Management - The International Perspective: For coordinating the humanitarian assistance provided and the relief efforts of the international agencies and the United Nations agencies, the UN General Assembly has created the Office of the Emergency Relief Coordinator (ERC). The ERC reports to the UN Secretary-General and is assisted and represented by the in-country heads of the UN agencies called the UN Resident Coordinators (UNRCs). The ERC is the focal point in the UN System for disaster relief coordination, who is empowered by the UN General Assembly Resolution 2816 of 14 December 1971:

- The mobilize direct and coordinate the relief activities of various organizations of the UN system in response to a request for disaster assistance from the stricken State;
- To coordinate the UN assistance with assistance given by inter-governmental and non-governmental organizations, in particular by the International Cross;
- The receive, on behalf of the UN Secretary-General contributions offered to him for disaster relief assistance to be carried out by the UN, its agencies and programs for particular emergency situations;
- To assist the Government of the stricken country to assess its relief and other needs and to evaluate the priority of those needs, to disseminate that information to prospective donors and others concerned, and to serve as a clearing-house for assistance extended or planned by all sources of external aid.

Q2. Describe in brief the following disasters:

(i) Orrissa super cyclone- October 1999

Ans. The 1999 Odisha cyclone was the strongest recorded tropical cyclone in the North Indian Ocean and among the most destructive in the region. The 1999 Odisha cyclone organized into a tropical depression in the Andaman Sea on 25 October, though its origins could be traced back to an area of convection in the Sulu Sea four days prior. The disturbance gradually strengthened as it took a west-northwesterly path, reaching cyclonic storm strength the next day. Taking advantage of highly favorable conditions, the storm rapidly intensified, attaining super cyclonic storm intensity on 28 October, before peaking on the next day with winds of 260 km/h (160 mph) and a record-low pressure of 912 mbar. The storm maintained this intensity as it made landfall on Odisha on 29 October. The cyclone steadily weakened due to persistent land interaction and dry air, remaining quasi-stationary for two days before slowly drifting offshore as a much weaker system; the storm dissipated on 4 November over the Bay of Bengal.

(ii) Mozambique flood- February 2000

Ans. The 2000 Mozambique flood was a natural disaster that occurred in February and March 2000. The catastrophic flooding was caused by heavy rainfall that lasted for five weeks and made many homeless. Approximately 700 people were killed. 1,400 km^2 of arable land was affected and 20,000 herds of cattle were lost. It was the worst flood in Mozambique in 50 years.

It started in South Africa when heavy rain falls traveled over to Mozambique. It caused dozens of deaths. 44,000 were left homeless and many of them had lost relatives of some kind. Later, Cyclone Eline came and destroyed many more homes and lives. The women and children were hurrying to shelter and high land. 800 had died and thousands of livestock were killed. The government distributed 15 million dollars to its citizens to account for damage property and loss of income. As of 2016, people were still living in recovery shelters with fluctuating water supplies.

Q3. Elucidate the coordination of relief activities.

Ans. During and after any disaster/emergency, coordination of various relief activities (planning and procurement of supplies, following inventories, organizing and ensuring the distribution according to priorities and needs and continually sharing information) is an important though difficult and one of the challenging tasks. An emergency situation is characterized by overwhelming needs, competing priorities, destroyed or damaged communication and transportation infrastructure, a rapid influx of providers of humanitarian assistance coupled with an outburst of mutual aid from local citizens, and highly stressed local governmental and non-governmental institutions.

While coordination may not be easily defined, its absence is characterized by gaps in service to affected population; duplication of efforts; inappropriate assistance; inefficient use of resources; bottlenecks, impediments and slow reaction to changing conditions; and frustration of relief providers, officials and survivors - in general, an unsatisfactory response to the emergency.

Coordination is a result of intentional actions to harmonize individual responses to maximize impact and achieve synergy - a situation where the overall effect is greater than the sum of the parts. Coordination beings with the initiation of working relationships and regular sharing of information. As coordination increases there is a resulting change in the way relief providers (whether governmental or non-governmental) implement their programs of assistance. Since relief providers cooperate, individuals and organizations adapt and adjust their efforts based on changing needs and each other's strengths and weaknesses.

It could be recalled that along with the relief supplies sent by various State Governments, many voluntary agencies, business houses, inspired group of individuals rushed loads of relief supplies (drinking water bottles, clothing, temporary shelter materials, food grains etc.) to Bhuj.

Further, two and half years after the earthquake (June 2003), it is observed that the Indira Gandhi International Airports Authority is concerned over disposing off the consignments containing relief materials (old clothes, blankets etc.) sent by donors for the earthquake affected people in Gujarat.

Q4. Describe the health services in disasters. Also elaborate public health issues after disasters.

Ans. Health care workers have unique skills for handling all aspects of disasters. It includes assessment, priority setting, collaboration, and addressing both preventive and acute care needs. Health is one of the key objectives and a significant yardstick of success of effective disaster management during this stage. Health care is a critical determinant for survival in the initial stages of a disaster. Disasters almost always have significant impacts on the entire health sector. When it comes to disaster mitigation, preparedness and response, hospitals and health care professionals require special attention due to the vital functions they perform, their high level of occupancy and role they play during a disaster situation. The impacts could be direct on the health sector infrastructure such destruction or damage to the hospital building, loss of or injury to the health personnel, destruction or damage to the other infrastructure within the hospital building, pressure on the existing resource while dealing with a large number of sudden influx of patients etc. During a disaster, when the urgent survival needs including urgent medical care are met and mortality rates been declined by immediate mass causality management, a more comprehensive range of services are needed to be provided. Throughout all phase of a disaster, a systematic approach is needed to be developed to design, implement, monitor and evaluate these comprehensive services, which should ensure that most health needs are met with appropriate coverage, optimized access, and quality services.

Public Health Issues: Disasters have been contributing to the outbreak of some specific epidemic diseases as the disease transmission risk factors increase when a disaster hits a particular geographic area. Lack of clean water and the suspension of public health programmes, all help illnesses, such as cholera or dengue or malaria to multiply after natural disasters. Often these illnesses can be more deadly than the original disaster. Rapid changes in the human environment and health may occur also as a result of natural disasters or acts of war or of other man-made circumstances including major industrial accident. However, health problems arising out of the disasters may vary in types and degrees depending upon particular type of a disaster.

Types of disasters & proneness to different epidemics: The increased man-vector contact in precarious shelters and temporary camps and the disruption of control activities may be more important causes for epidemics after disasters caused by natural hazards. More importantly, disasters caused by natural hazards (hurricanes, floods, earthquakes, cyclones and volcanic eruptions) can contribute to the transmission of some diseases provided the causative agent is already in the environment. Although major health epidemics are rare in the aftermath of these disasters, but some disasters are so great that large numbers of the population are displaced, creating perfect conditions for the spread of disease.

While earthquakes, avalanches, and landslides may result in enteric epidemics due to improper water supply and sanitation; volcanic eruption can lead to respiratory epidemic; and unprecedented amounts of rain leading to disastrous flooding flood and flash floods, and cyclone can result in pneumonia as well as other waterborne communicable diseases. In the period immediately following a hurricane, the risk of acquiring malaria, dengue or encephalitis may decrease as a result of the destruction of breeding places of the local vectors. Viral agents during the time of nuclear, biological and chemical warfare can cause disease like anthrax, vibrio cholera, and plague requiring immediate treatment.

However, it is important to remember that epidemics do not spontaneously occur after a natural disaster. The more likely cause of disease is the lack of potable water and adequate sanitation. In country like India where cholera is prevalent, general assumption is that disease will spread after any disaster affecting water supply, food quality and sanitation. However, the health problems in natural as well as man-made disasters could be due to either or any combination of factors enumerated below:

- Directly due to impact of disasters like drowning during floods, multiple injuries during earthquakes, thermal blast and radiation effects during and after nuclear disaster and large number of injuries after civil unrest.
- Due to non or inadequate availability of immediate medical care.
- Due to delay in evacuation and transportation to advanced medical centers.
- Due to mass shelter, water shortage and contamination, unhygienic living conditions leading to outbreaks of communicable diseases and resulting in epidemics, another health disaster.

The main causes of disease: Population movement, poor sanitation, water contamination and the interruption of public health programmes are the main reasons for the spread of disease after natural and humanitarian disasters. Often displaced populations are forced to gather in confined spaces, further enabling the spread of epidemics, such as cholera, malaria and dengue fever. According to the World Health Organization, the presence of dead bodies is not a major factor in the spread of communicable diseases.

The spread of cholera is one of the main dangers following a natural disaster. Cholera is an acute infection of the gut, which causes chronic diarrhoea and vomiting. This can lead to severe dehydration and, in some extreme cases, death. However, most people who are infected by the bug do not become ill and 90% of those who do are only mildly or moderately ill. Cholera is spread by contaminated water and food. Sudden outbreaks, such as those, which follow a disaster, are usually caused by a contaminated water supply. The bug is most deadly when it arrives unexpectedly - as in times of disaster - because there are often no facilities for treatment or because people cannot get treatment in time. In communities, which are unprepared for a cholera outbreak, up to 50% of people who become seriously ill may die. Cholera can be effectively treated with oral rehydration salts and antibiotics. Containing a cholera outbreak involves ensuring there are proper sanitation methods for disposing of sewage, an adequate drinking water supply and good food hygiene.

Flooding is the most common type of natural disaster worldwide, accounting for an estimated 40% of all natural disasters. In riverine flooding, water levels can rise to flood stage gradually or very rapidly (i.e., flash flood) from snow melt or heavy or repeated rains. During the 1993 mid-western flood disaster, both gradual and flash flooding occurred.

Flash flooding is the leading cause of weather-related mortality in the United States (accounting for approximately 200 deaths per year). However, the public health impact of floods also includes damage or destruction to homes and displacement of the occupants that may, in turn, facilitate the spread of some infectious diseases because of crowded living conditions and compromised personal hygiene (i.e., hand washing). Stress-related mental health or substance-abuse problems may be associated with flood disasters. As the findings in this report indicate, medical and public health services may be interrupted in affected communities. Finally, the occurrence of injuries may increase during the clean-up phase of a disaster.

The multiple environmental consequences of flooding can directly affect the public's health. For example, water sources can become contaminated with faecal material or toxic chemicals, water or sewer systems can be disrupted, dangerous substances can be released (e.g., propane from damaged storage tanks), and solid-waste collection and disposal can be disrupted. In addition, flooding can result in vectorassociated problems, including increases in mosquito populations that, under certain circumstances, increase the risk for some mosquitoborne infectious diseases (e.g., viral encephalitis).

Floods and other natural disasters often are followed by rumors of epidemics (e.g., typhoid, cholera, or rabies) or unusual conditions such as increased snake or dog bites. Such unsubstantiated reports can gain public credibility when printed in newspapers or reported on television or radio as facts. The potential for such rumors underscores the need for valid and systematically collected data and the importance of basic public health surveillance in such settings. Elements to be considered in such surveillance efforts are described in the CDC publication Beyond the Flood: A Prevention Guide for Personal Health and Safety, which emphasizes the importance of (1) purification of drinking and cooking water; (2) disinfection of wells; (3) food safety (i.e., handling of food that may have come in contact with flood water or of refrigerated food after the interruption of electrical power); (4) sanitation and personal hygiene; (5) injury-prevention measures to be taken during the return to and cleaning up of flooded homes; (6) communicable diseases and vaccinations; (7) mosquito control; and (8) other hazards such as animals, chemicals, and swift-flowing water. Copies of the guide are available from state health departments.

Q5. What is the meaning of mass causality incidents (MCIs)? What are the various approaches of MCIs?

Or

Write down the different approaches of MCIs.

Ans. A mass casualty incident (often shortened to MCI and sometimes called a multiple-casualty incident or multiple-casualty situation) is any incident in which emergency medical services resources, such as personnel and equipment, are overwhelmed by the number and severity of casualties. For example, an incident where a two-person crew is responding to a motor vehicle collision with three severely injured people could be considered a mass casualty incident. The general public more commonly recognizes events such as building collapses train and bus collisions, plane crashes, earthquakes and other large-scale emergencies as mass casualty incidents. Events such as the Oklahoma City bombing in 1995 and the September 11 attacks in 2001 are well-publicized examples of mass casualty incidents. The most common types of MCIs are generally caused by terrorism, mass-transportation accidents, or natural disasters.

Different approaches to mass casualty incidents are as follows:

(1) Basic approach: A "scoop and run" method is used most commonly to deal with accident victims. This approach does not require specific technical ability from the rescuers. While this method can be justified for the management of small numbers of victims in certain circumstances (e.g., when an accident occurs in the immediate proximity of available emergency care services), the same approach in a mass casualty situation will result in the transfer of the problem from the incident site to the hospital, overwhelming and disrupting the care capacity of the health facility.

(2) Classical care approach: In the "classical care approach", first responders are trained to provide victims with basic triage and Held care before evacuation to the nearest available receiving health care facility.

This approach juxtaposes two organizations which are working independently with only weak linkages:

The field (often involving non-health sector responders), and

The receiving health care organization that is often totally divorced from the pre-hospital problem.

In a mass casualty situation, this approach will quickly result in chaos.

(3) Mass casualty management approach: Mass casualty management, the most sophisticated approach, includes preestablished procedures for resource mobilization, field management and hospital reception. It is based on specific training of various level of responders and incorporates links between field and health care facilities through a command post. It acknowledges the need for a multi-sectoral response for triage, field stabilization and evacuation to adapted health care facilities. The development of this approach was based on the availability of large amounts of human and material resources ("adequate manpower and equipment").

Attempting to replicate this approach in a country with limited resources does not result in the expected level of effectiveness. In such situations, the mass casualty management approach should be adapted with special attention given to a country's specific situational problems.

Actually in a mass casualty incident a small number of victims will need immediate treatment in a hospital, however, to reduce the mortality and morbidity the role of specifically skilled field level teams is very important. The success of a quick and effective mass casualty management depends largely on:

(i) Good triage capacity of the specifically trained field level teams;

(ii) Good radio-communication between field and hospital staff, and;

(iii) Good overall coordinated preparedness of the health sector along with other supporting sectors.

Thus, the concept of triage plays a significant role in the success of the management of victims of a MCI.

Triage is the process of determining the priority of patients' treatments based on the severity of their condition. This rations patient treatment efficiently when resources are insufficient for all to be treated immediately. The term comes from the French verb trier, meaning to separate, sift or select.[1] Triage may result in determining the order and priority of emergency treatment, the order and priority of emergency transport, or the transport destination for the patient.

Triage may also be used for patients arriving at the emergency department, or telephoning medical advice systems,[2] among others. This article deals with the concept of triage as it occurs in medical emergencies, including the prehospital setting, disasters, and emergency department treatment.

The field triage process could be done at three levels:

(i) On-site triage is done at the disaster site and the victims categorisation is done "where they are lying" ideally by using some colour code tags to reduce the incorrect classification. This is done primarily by the first responders, disaster response forces, emergency medical technicians and search and rescue workers. These trained personnel categorize victims into "acute" (red and yellow tags) and "not acute" (green and black tags). Generally, the acute victims are tied up with a red floating ribbon and the not acute victims with green ribbon to make it easier for the stretcher bearer to shift to victims to their designated places. This helps in reducing the on-site triage time to assess, categorize, mark and transport the victims to the nearest point/location where advance medical care facilities are available.

(ii) **Medical triage** is primarily done by a team of experienced medical personnel at the point/location where advance medical care facilities are available. The objective of medical triage is to determine the type and level of medical care needed by the victims. The triage team is consisted of an anesthesiologist, emergency physician, surgeons, a gynecologist and obstetrician, and if possible a pediatrician. Accordingly, red (victims needing immediate stabilization care such as victims having respiratory distress, major internal or external bleeding, shock, head injury), yellow (victims requiring close monitoring and can be somewhat delayed such as victims with risk of shock-heart attack or major abdominal trauma, compound fractures, severe burns), green (victims requiring delayed or no treatment such as victims with minor fractures, wounds, burns), and black (for deceased) colour categories can be assigned to the victims. However, depending on the resources available and magnitude of the MCI, the triage can be done. For example, a victim with 50-60% burn injuries can be tagged with red band if the incident is small and resources are available in the health care facilities, and the same victim can wait for an hour (yellow tag) in a major MCI if the victim has no respiratory distress.

(iii) **Evacuation triage** is primarily done to prioritize victims needing transfer by equipped ambulance with medical escort to other tertiary care level hospital with very advanced level of health care facilities available. Here the classification of victims is also done following the colour codes, but the criteria chosen may differ from the medical triage. For example, the victims needing life saving surgery, function saving surgery and ICU facilities such as ventilator, advance monitoring of cardio-vascular functions are tagged with red bands, while the victims needing major surgeries but not really life threatening could be tagged with yellow bands. The objective is to evacuate the victims from the advance health facilities, where the medical triage is done to transfer them with BLS ambulances to the tertiary care hospitals.

Q6. Discuss the psycho-social and mental health issues after disasters. Also explain in brief the institutional mechanism for disaster health care management and national guidelines on medical preparedness and mass causality management.

Or

Disaster-affected people experience various psychological reactions. Discuss.

Or

What are the national guidelines on medical preparedness and mass casuality management?

Or

Write down the institutional mechanism for disaster health care management.

Ans. Disaster-affected people experience various psychological reactions. Emotional instability, stress reactions, anxiety, trauma and other psychological symptoms are observed commonly after the disaster and other traumatic experiences. These psychological effects have a massive impact on the concerned individual and also on communities. These reactions immediately follow the event while socio-economic impacts like lack of employment; homelessness, environmental destruction and disorganisation emerge as a consequence following the devastation caused by the disaster.

After a disaster, the emotional reaction among members of a community may vary from the other and this also usually undergoes change over time depending upon the coping capacity and socio-economic condition of that community. Therefore, post-disaster psychological interventions should be flexible and based on an ongoing assessment of needs. The emotional reactions should be understood based on the manifestation of various stress reactions, level of effort put by the people for their own reconstruction, the pattern and amount of disability created due to these psychological stress etc. Some factors that could influence the reactions among people are nature and severity of the disaster, amount of exposure to the disaster, availability of adequate social support, age, gender, status of the person (single, widowed, married), separation/displacement from locality, separation from family/primary support group, personal losses of the survivor (loss of kith and kin, property, source of livelihood, personal injury.

Institutional Mechanism for Disaster Health Care Management: Most of the disaster situation is to be managed at State and District levels. The centre plays a supporting role and provides assistance when the consequences of disaster exceed district and State capacities. The centre mobilizes support in terms of providing emergency teams, support personnel, specialized equipments and operating facilities depending on the scale of the disaster and the need of the State and District.

Health is a state subject in India and the states have a three-tier system of service and health facility provision to the citizens, which consists of primary health care facilities at village level, district level, district level hospitals and tertiary care hospitals at state level. National Health Policy and programmes are also implemented by states. Thus, the health care service organisations extend from national to village level.

At the national level, the Ministry of Health and Family Welfare (MoH&FW) has been assigned the legislative capacity for a number of health care subject spanned from medical to dental, nursing, pharmacy, mental health, standardisation of drugs, Ayurveda, Yoga & Naturopathy, Unani, Siddha and Homoeophaty (AYUSH), and epidemic prevention and control. It has two departments, health and family welfare and AYUSH. The Emergency Medical Response (EMR) division of the technical wing of the Directorate General of Health Services (DGHS) is the focal point for implementing the Emergency Support Function (ESF) plan that includes identification of nodal officers for coordination, crisis management committee and quick response teams at head quarter and field level, resource inventory, etc. the decision making body is the Crisis Management Group under the Secretary, Health and Family Welfare, which is advised by the Technical Advisor Committee under DGHS.

Medical and paramedical personnel in (1) tertiary care institutes runs by MoH&FW and (2) available with central government health scheme could become useful for medical team deployment and mobilisation in case of mass casualty incidents. Similarly for public personnel can be deputed from the National Institute of Communicable Diseases (NICD), All India Institute of Hygiene and public Health (AIHPH) and other

ICMR institutes. For investigating outbreaks, NICD is the Nodal agency, which provides teaching/training, research and laboratory support.

However, health is a state subject under the present constitutional provisions. The administrative responsibility of medical preparedness and mass casualty management primarily remains with the state health departments. State health department is structured as three-tier system comprising of PHCs and CHCs at block levels, district hospitals at district level and tertiary care hospitals/medical institutions at state headquarters/major cities. With wide variation with multiplicity of agencies/departments that run these systems in different states, these institutions are normally overwhelmed with the routine load and their surge capacity is limited. Therefore, capacity development of these institutions at all three levels for catering to mass casualty incidents is a great challenge, hence, needs-urgent attention from all role players, both Government and Private working in the health sector development planning.

National Guidelines on Medical Preparedness and Mass Casualty Management: It has been accepted that morbidity, mortality and mental health effects of disasters can be reduced and mitigated through proper measures. Therefore, keeping the gravity of the health risk posed by disasters, medical preparedness needs to encompass all the issues related to health and related effects as a consequences of disasters and their aftermath. In addition to trauma and suffering, these may also result in a long-term deleterious impact on the mental health status of the affected community.

National Disaster Management Authority, Government of India has developed these guidelines. Under Section-6 of the Disaster Management Act, 2005 of Government of India, the National Disaster Management Authority (NDMA) is Inter alia mandated to issue guidelines for preparing action plans for holistic and coordinated management of all disasters. The guidelines on medical preparedness and mass casualty management focus on all aspects of medical preparedness and mass casualty management with emphasis on mitigation, preparedness, relief and response. These guidelines have documented important preparatory measures which, though already existing, require definite up gradation both qualitatively and quantitatively. Latest best practices and concepts in the medical and scientific field have also been included, which may be adopted, based upon the area and need assessment analyses. These guidelines also provide important baseline information to various planners and implementers regarding different specialized facilities and methodologies required for effective implementation of health impacts of chemical, biological, radiological and nuclear disasters.

The effective implementation of these guidelines can be achieved with the collective action of all stakeholders, particularly State Governments (Especially Department of Health & Family Welfare & District Administration) and their Disaster Management Authorities.

Q7. Describe Hospital Disaster Management Plan (HDMP).

Ans. A Hospital Disaster Management Plan is a simple comprehensive and well defined hospital disaster/emergency/crisis management activities framework prepared by a particular hospital to handle disasters/emergencies to minimize the loss of human beings and limbs, to prevent deterioration of injuries and sufferings of the survivors and to function as a life service centre during the disasters. It considers the management protocol for both internal and external disasters, which may affect the functioning of the hospital.

The type of disaster/emergency/crisis situations hospitals may have to face are mainly:

(1) Mass Casualty incidents due to natural or man-made causes;

(2) Public Health Emergencies: Such emergencies may primarily be outbreak of infectious diseases or an after effect of natural disaster with its after effects on the Public health; and

(3) Crisis situation related to Nuclear, Biological Chemical and Radiological attacks.

The prime objective of Hospital Disaster Management Plan is to ensure mitigation and preparedness measures that have to be taken up by hospitals (irrespective of bed strength, locality, human and material resources) *for prompt and well coordinated effective response framework for either internal or external disasters faced by the hospitals.*

Therefore each hospital in Delhi and NCR Region must follow the HDMP template, however may modify the plan keeping its own organizational structure, human and material resources and equipments in view. However, this is mandatory for each hospital to have:

(i) A written plan clearly mentioning the step by step approach to be followed by the hospital in case of disaster/emergency/crisis situations.

(ii) A written plan regarding hospital safety mitigation measures, such as structural and non-structural mitigation measures that can be done to ensure safe hospital.

(iii) A written plan for people/teams/committees responsible for management of disasters, their roles, functions and chain of command.

(iv) A written plan for communication channels and methods of dissemination of information to the hospital staff and to the public.

(v) A written framework for plan activation protocol for different disasters/emergency situations

(vi) A written plan for hospital's protocol for capacity building (training and retraining) of hospital staff in various aspects of disaster health care management.

The above mentioned features highlight the composition of a hospital disaster management plan. This is also important to note that the plan prepared by the hospital needs to be tested at regular intervals through Mock Drills (Table Top and Field Level) and the schedule for the same is to made explicit in the document. The document must be made available to all sections of the hospital staff working in outpatient, clinical, support services, and to the regulatory authorities.

Q8. What is the meaning of incident command system (ICS)? Explain its basic features.

Ans. The Incident Command System (ICS) is a standardized approach to the command, control, and coordination of emergency response providing a common hierarchy within which responders from multiple agencies can be effective.

ICS was initially developed to address problems of inter-agency responses to wildfires in California and Arizona but is now a component of the National Incident Management System (NIMS) in the US, where it has evolved into use in All-Hazards situations, ranging from active shootings to Hazmat scenes. In addition, ICS has acted as a pattern for similar approaches internationally.

The ICS concept was formed in 1968 at a meeting of Fire Chiefs in Phoenix, Arizona. The program was built primarily to take after the management hierarchy of the US Navy and it was mainly for firefighting of wildfires in California and Arizona. During the 1970s, ICS was fully developed during massive wildfire suppression efforts in California (FIRESCOPE) that followed a series of catastrophic wildfires, starting with the massive Laguna fire in 1970. Property damage ran into the millions, and many people died or were injured. Studies determined that response problems often related to communication and management deficiencies rather than lack of resources or failure of tactics.

Some of the following are basic features of ICS:

Unity of command: Each individual participating in the operation reports to only one supervisor. This eliminates the potential for individuals to receive conflicting orders from a variety of supervisors, thus increasing accountability, preventing freelancing, improving the flow of information, helping with the coordination of operational efforts, and enhancing operational safety. This concept is fundamental to the ICS chain of command structure.

Common terminology: Individual response agencies previously developed their protocols separately, and subsequently developed their terminology separately. This can lead to confusion as a word may have a different meaning for each organization.

When different organizations are required to work together, the use of common terminology is an essential element in team cohesion and communications, both internally and with other organizations responding to the incident.

An incident command system promotes the use of a common terminology and has an associated glossary of terms that help bring consistency to position titles, the description of resources and how they can be organized, the type and names of incident facilities, and a host of other subjects. The use of common terminology is most evident in the titles of command roles, such as Incident Commander, Safety Officer or Operations Section Chief.

Management by objective: Incidents are managed by aiming towards specific objectives. Objectives are ranked by priority; should be as specific as possible; must be attainable; and if possible given a working time-frame. Objectives are accomplished by first outlining strategies (general plans of action), then determining appropriate tactics (how the strategy will be executed) for the chosen strategy.

Flexible and modular organization: Incident Command structure is organized in such a way as to expand and contract as needed by the incident scope, resources and hazards. Command is established in a top-down fashion, with the most important and authoritative positions established first. For example, Incident Command is established by the first arriving unit.

Only positions that are required at the time should be established. In most cases, very few positions within the command structure will need to be activated. For example, a single fire truck at a dumpster fire will have the officer filling the role of IC, with no other roles required. As more trucks get added to a larger incident, more roles will be delegated to other officers and the Incident Commander (IC) role will probably be handed to a more-senior officer.

Only in the largest and most complex operations would the full ICS organization be staffed. Conversely, as an incident scales down, roles will be merged back up the tree until there is just the IC role remaining.

Span of control: To limit the number of responsibilities and resources being managed by any individual, the ICS requires that any single person's span of control should be between three and seven individuals, with five being ideal. In other words, one manager should have no more than seven people working under them at any given time. If more than seven resources are being managed by an individual, then they are being overloaded and the command structure needs to be expanded by delegating responsibilities (e.g. by defining new sections, divisions, or task forces). If fewer than three, then the position's authority can probably be absorbed by the next highest rung in the chain of command.

Incident Action Plans: Incident Action Plans (IAPs) ensure that everyone is working in concert toward the same goals set for that operational period by providing all incident supervisory personnel with direction for actions to be taken during the operational period identified in the plan. Incident Action Plans provide a coherent means of communicating the overall incident objectives for both operational and support activities. They include measurable strategic objectives to be achieved in a time frame called an Operational Period, which may be any interval of time but is commonly 12 hours. They may be verbal or written except for hazardous material incidents where it must be written, and are prepared by the Planning Section.

The consolidated IAP is a very important component of the ICS that reduces freelancing and ensures a coordinated response. At the simplest level, all Incident Action Plans must have four elements:

- What do we want to do?
- Who is responsible for doing it?
- How do we communicate with each other?
- What is the procedure if someone is injured?

The content of the IAP is organized by a number of standardized ICS forms that allow for accurate and precise documentation of an incident.

Comprehensive resource management: Comprehensive resource management is a key management principle that implies that all assets and personnel during an event need to be tracked and accounted for. It can also include processes for reimbursement for resources, as appropriate. Resource management includes processes for:

- Categorizing resources.
- Ordering resources.
- Dispatching resources.
- Tracking resources.
- Recovering resources.

Comprehensive resource management ensures that visibility is maintained over all resources so they can be moved quickly to support the preparation and response to an incident, and ensuring a graceful demobilization. It also applies to the classification of resources by type and kind, and the categorization of resources by their status.

- Assigned resources are those that are working on a field assignment under the direction of a supervisor.
- Available resources are those that are ready for deployment(staged), but have not been assigned to a field assignment.
- Out-of-service resources are those that are not in either the "available" or "assigned" categories. Resources can be "out-of-service" for a variety of reasons including: resupplying after a

sortie (most common), shortfall in staffing, personnel taking a rest, damaged or inoperable.

T-Cards (ICS 219, Resource Status Card) are most commonly used to track these resources. The cards are placed in T-Card racks located at an Incident Command Post for easy updating and visual tracking of resource status.

Integrated Communications: Developing an integrated voice and data communications system, including equipment, systems, and protocols, must occur prior to an incident.

Effective ICS communications include three elements:

- Modes: The "hardware" systems that transfer information.
- Planning: Planning for the use of all available communications resources.
- Networks: The procedures and processes for transferring information internally and externally.

Q9. What are the primary functions of incident command system (ICS)?

Ans. Primary functions of incident command system (ICS) are describe below:

(1) Command Staff and General Staff

Command Staff: The command staff in ICS consists of Incident Commander who has the overall responsibility for managing an incident and three other positions namely Information Officer, Safety Officer and Liaison Officer. The Information Officer is responsible for developing and releasing information to the news media, incident personnel or any other appropriate agencies and organization. The Liaison officer is generally appointed in incident involving several agencies or which are multi-jurisdictional in nature and the primary responsibility of Liaison officer is to bring coordination with various agencies, which are either directly assisting or cooperating agencies i.e. providing non-critical resources to incident management. The Safety officer's function is to develop and recommend measures for assuring personnel safety of incident personnel (responders). The Safety officer if needed can exercise the authority to directly stop unsafe operation if the conditions are life threatening for the responders.

General Staff: The ICS General staff consists of the following positions and those working under these sections:

(A) Operation Section Chief

(B) Planning Section Chief

(C) Logistics Section Chief

(D) Finance and Administration Section Chief

The principle ICS functions

Command: The Incident Commander (IC) has overall responsibility for all functions and this person may elect to perform all functions or delegate some of them to other positions. Thus while other position in any ICS team may or may not be filled depending on incident size and need, there will always be an IC. If need be, a Deputy Incident Commander is also appointed who may be from the same agency as that of IC from assisting agencies with same level of competence so that he or she can take over the role of IC if such a situation arises.

The major duties and responsibilities of Incident Commander include; determine incident objectives and priorities, establish Incident Command Post, establish Incident Command Organization, ensure planning meeting, approve incident action plan, coordinate activities of command and general staff, keep informed responsible official about incident status, authorize release of information to the media and ensure that adequate safety measures are in place.

Operations: The Operation Section is responsible for managing and directing all tactical action to meet incident objectives. The Operation section consists of the following components; ground or surface based tactical resources, aviation resources e.g. helicopter, fixed wing aircrafts etc. and staging areas. The resources which under the ground or surface based can be organized under three ways; single resources, strike teams and task forces, depending on the application area and tactical requirements. Many incidents require deployment of aviation resources and in such case ICS recommends establishment of a separate branch in the Operation Section for aviation resources. The concept of staging areas in ICS refers to a temporary location for placing resources which are available for incident assignment. The location should be sufficiently close to the incident site of deployment so that resources placed there can be at the site of assignment/operation within three to five minutes. Several staging areas can be set up within an incident and the main purpose is to ensure planned operational time is not lost on account of resource readiness and deployment.

Planning: The Planning section is responsible for the collection, evaluation and display of incident information, maintaining statues of resources, preparing incident action plan and incident related documentation. There are four units in the planning section that can be activated as and when required. These units are:

- **Resource Unit:** This unit is responsible for maintaining the status of all resources (primary and support) at an incident. It achieves this through overseeing the check-in processes of all resources, maintain aces of a master list of all resources e.g. key supervisory personnel, crucial resources etc. and developing a status keeping system to display status of resources, their assignment position etc.
- **Situation Unit:** The situation unit is responsible for collection, processing and organizing of all situation related information. They also prepare future projection and likely scenario for the planning purpose. The unit can engage three other position namely filed observer, display processor i.e. for information display and weather observer.
- **Documentation Unit:** This unit is responsible for the maintenances of accurate and up to date incident files. Such documentation is necessary either for incident management, legal, analytical or historical purpose.
- **Demobilisation Unit:** The demobilisation unit is responsible for developing a demobilisation plan. In large or complex incident such a plan is essential for efficient use of resources.

Technical specialists: Certain incidents may require use of technical specialists who have specialized knowledge and expertise such as meteorologists, hydrologists, GIS specialists etc. Such technical specialists generally work in the Planning Section, often associated with situation unit or any other units as required for example, if such a specialist's expertise is primarily with resource inventory then the specialists can be associated with resource unit or if the incident it handling hazardous material, a special unit for such specialists may be created in the planning section.

Logistics: The Logistics section provides support for services and support to incident management. The primary functions of Logistics section is to provide support for incident facilities e.g. base, camp etc., transportation, communication, food services, ground transportation, medical services and ordering resources. In large incidents requiring huge quantity of resources or in a fully expanded logistics section, the following six units may be established.

- **Supply Unit:** This unit is responsible for ordering, receiving, processing and storing all incident related resources from outside. This unit is different from resource unit in the planning section on the ground that resource unit do not order any resource, which in itself is a specialized task e.g. identification of sources, quality check, transportation etc. The resource unit on the other hand oversees arrival of resources and prepares their status summary etc. for planning section whereas the supply unit in Logistics section takes the responsibility of ordering, receiving, processing resources. The Supply Unit can engage ordering Manager and Receiving/Distribution Manager for this function.
- **Facilities Unit:** This unit is responsible for establishing, maintainaces and demobilisation of all incident related facilities except staging areas. These facilities include Incident Command Post from where the command staff function, Incident Base and Camp where there will be provision for rest, food, water, sanitation, medical facilities etc or any other such facilities for incident personnel. The basic difference between a Base and Camp is that Base is a much better arrangement compared to camp and in an incident there can be several camps depending on the incident area. The unit also ensures security for various facilities in a incident.
- **Ground Support Unit:** The Ground support unit is responsible for the maintainaces. service and fuelling of all mobile equipments and vehicles with the exception of aviation resources. The aviation resources come under air operation branch in the Operation Section. The Ground support unit also has the responsibility for ground transportation of personnel, supplies equipments and for developing and incident traffic plan.
- **Communication Unit:** The Unit is responsible for developing the plan for incident communication equipment and facilities,

installation and testing of communication equipments, supervision of communication centre and distribution and maintainaces of communication equipments.

- **Food Unit:** The Unit is in charge of providing food needs for the entire incident including all remote location; camp, staging areas etc.
- **Medical Unit:** The medical unit is responsible for providing medical services for all incident assigned personnel. The unit is to develop an incident medical plan identifying various medical service centers, ambulances, procedures.

This needs to be noted here that the food and medical unit in the Logistics section are primarily meant for incident personnel and not for incident affected public which is to be taken care by the operation section.

Finance and Administration: This section is responsible for tracking incident related costs, personnel and equipment records, procurement contracts etc. Not all incidents will require separate Finance and Administration section or a fully expanded Finance/Administration section but depending on the incident need such as size of the incident, agencies involved, type of resources etc. The various units of the section can be activated or deactivated. There are four units in the Finance/Administration section:

- **Time Unit:** The unit is responsible for ensuring accurate recording of personnel time and compliance with specific agencies time-recording policies
- **Procurement Unit:** All financial matters related to vendor contracts, leases and financial agreements. The unit is also responsible for maintaining equipment time records.
- **Compensation/Claim Unit:** The Unit oversees all formalities for completion of all forms for incident personnel and local agencies. The claim unit is responsible for investigating all claims involved with the incident.
- **Cost unit:** The primary function of this unit is to provide all incident cost analysis. It ensures that proper identification of all equipment and personnel requiring payments, records all cost data, analyze and prepare estimate of cost and maintain record of incident cost.

Q10. How does ICS work?

Ans. Any incident, be it a natural disaster or any other emergencies is first to be notified that ICS will be used and an Incident Command/Management Team is to be made in charge for its management. Depending on the size and nature of the incident, the Incident Commander will appoint other ICS team position. The six sequential steps involved in planning process are:

- ***Understand the Situation*:** Some of the key questions in this will be, what has happened, what progress has been made, what is the incident growth potential, what actions have been taken, how effective have been the current plan, what is the present and future resource capability etc. A full understanding of the incident is essential especially the special characteristics of such incidents.
- ***Establish Incident Objectives and Strategies*:** The three main characteristics of good objectives are that they should be attainable, measurable and flexible. The strategy should address various considerations such as practical, suitable, within acceptable safety limits, consistent with sound environmental practices and should meet political consideration. There should always be alternative strategies to meet incident objective assuming the risk of failure for any specific strategy. In small incident, the IC may determine the objectives and strategies but in large incident the general staff also contribute to objectives and strategies development.
- ***Determine Tactical Direction and Make Resource Management:*** The next step in this process is to determine tactical direction based on selected strategy and assign appropriate resources. The tactical direction is planned for an operational period which will have clear, realistic and measureable objectives that can be accomplished within that operational period. If required resources are not available, then necessary adjustments have to be made in the operational period objectives or in some cases a reassessment of strategies taking into account resource availability. At the same time, personnel and logistical support factor must also be considered before finalizing the tactical and strategies.

- ***Prepare the Incident Action Plan:*** The planning meeting (and if required a pre-planning meeting to resolve contentious issues) is conducted with participation of key members of ICS team such as Incident Commander, Planning Section Chief, Operation Section Chief, Logistics Section Chief, Finance/Administration Section Chief, Resource Unit Leader, Safety Officer and Agency Representative etc. or any other member as necessary to finalize the incident action plan.
- ***Implement the Plan:*** Once the incident action plan is prepared and approved by the Incident Commander, there is a general briefing for all the assigned incident personnel and also specific briefing for selected section. They copy of the plan is circulated to concerned staff and according to the plan, action is initiated
- ***Evaluation of the Plan:*** To ensure that the plan is effective, three steps are taken. Firstly before approving and releasing the plan Incident Commander can circulate the plan to general staff e.g. various section chiefs to review and assess if the plan reflects the current situation. Secondly during the operational period the Incident commander or operation section chief and planning section chief regularly monitor the progress against agreed objective to detect deficiencies and if required take corrective measures and thirdly the operation section chief can make expedient changes to tactical operation in the action plan if necessary to achieve incident objectives. While a particular operational period is in progress, planning for the next operational period starts.

Q11. Write a short note on ICS in India.

Ans. Based on the recommendation of High Powered Committee (HPC) report, Government of India has decided for adapting of ICS to suit Indian system of administration and institutionalizing it gradually for professionalizing disaster response. Accordingly the National Institute of Disaster Management, New Delhi, Lal Bahadur Shastri National Academy of Administration, Mussoorie and Six Regional Centers have been designated for adapting, training and institutionalizing ICS in India. It is important to note here that the approach in India has been not to replace the Indian system of emergency management which has come through a long period of evolution keeping in consideration local condition. But the idea is to strengthen this system with ICS by suitable modification wherever there are gaps. The ICS adaptation process is underway since 2003 and during this time large number of personnel from various Central government departments, State Government, NGO, National Disaster Response Force, Civil Defense etc. have been trained on ICS. Some of these trained personnel have also tried to apply ICS during actual emergencies such as Flood, Tsunami, Festivals etc. in different parts of the country. To take this process further, there have been pilotings of ICS model in some of the most vulnerable districts of three states; Gujarat, Assam and Andhra Pradesh. In these pilot districts, District incident management teams have been formed, trained in adapted ICS model and to be deployed during any emergency. These experiments are to be tried out at state and national level in due course. Similarly for providing policy support, National Disaster Management Authority has recommended implementation of ICS model response in many of its hazard guidelines.

Chapter-4

Recovery and Reconstruction

Q1. Highlight the concept of damage and loss assessment.

Or

Define damage assessment and list the objectives of assessment.

Or

What are the guiding principles which regulate the assessment of damage and losses?

Or

Write a short note on 'post-disaster assessments'.

Ans. Post-disaster assessments can be broadly divided into two parts viz. situation assessment and needs assessment. Situation assessment focuses on the situation on the ground, depicting the magnitude and impact of the disaster on the affected population and infrastructure. Needs assessment articulates the level and type of assistance required for the population affected by the disaster and focuses on "what needs to be done" for relief, reconstruction and rehabilitation. The assessment process therefore covers the nature and extent of a disaster, priority needs of the affected community, particularly of the affected people.

While damage and loss assessments provide broad information about the impact of disaster on people, infrastructure and the economy, needs assessment helps to understand the type of assistance required for the affected population. Each of them is important to initiate design and management of reconstruction programs.

Damage refers to the impact on lives and the physical assets affected in a disaster. It assesses direct costs like buildings, livelihood, agriculture and animal husbandry, services (educational, health and recreational facilities), infrastructure and utilities (water supply, roads, sewerage, bridges, electricity, telecommunication, etc.)

Losses refer to the changes in economic flows caused by disaster. It assesses direct income loss and indirect losses, which are costs related to changes in production, operation, delays, etc due to the disaster. Losses continue to occur until the desired reconstruction process is complete.

Damage assessment is an important tool for retrospective and prospective analysis of disasters to assimilate the extent of impact of a disaster. This forms the basis for future disaster preparedness and preventive planning. It is essential in determining: what happened, what the effects were, which areas were hardest hit, what situations must be given priority and what types of assistance are needed, for example, Local, State, or Union? Emergency response can be more effective, equipment and personnel can be better used, and help can be provided quicker if a thorough damage assessment is performed beforehand.

The Federal Emergency Management Agency (FEMA), the nodal agency of the United States defines damage assessment as "The process used to appraise or determine the number of injuries and deaths, damage to public and private property, and the status of key facilities and services such as hospitals and other health care facilities, fire and police stations, communications networks, water and sanitation systems, utilities, and transportation networks resulting from a manmade or natural disaster."

The basic objectives of damage assessment could be summarised as follows:

- To make a rapid assessment of areas affected to know the extent of impact for purpose of immediate rescue and relief operations;
- To prepare estimates for the amount of relief to be provided and the mode of relief, be it food, clothing, medicines, shelter or other essential commodities;
- To make a detailed assessment regarding requirements for long-term relief and rehabilitation planning; and

- To identify focus areas for the purpose of 'retrofitting' actions in similar future situations.

A clear procedure and protocol of damage assessment is imperative in order to ensure that the system is:

- Transparent- so that the assessment procedures can be followed easily;
- Consistent and standardized to enable meaningful comparisons;
- Replicable- to enable the assessments to be checked
- Based on economic principles- so that assessed losses represent properly the real losses to the economy.
- Documented in such a way that the approach can be easily checked or modified in the light of new information. This also ensures transparency and accountability.

Guiding Principles: The internationally followed guiding principles for assessment include the following:

- **Needs and local priorities:** identifying without discrimination on the basis of political, religious, ethnic or gender considerations;
- **Subsidiarity:** designing and implementation at the lowest competent tier of government for each reconstruction activity;
- **Consultation:** empowering local communities and stakeholders to make their own decisions during recovery, and participate fully in reconstruction activities;
- **Communication and transparency:** strengthening mechanisms to ensure access to information regarding policies, entitlements, implementation procedures, and regular feedback and grievance redress to implementing authorities;
- **Vulnerability:** reducing future vulnerability through a multi-hazard risk approach;
- **Coordination:** ensuring a coordinated approach to prevent duplication or an overlap in activities.

Q2. What is the process of assessment? Write down the methodology for assessing the loss and damage.

Or

What are the various methodologies used to assess the damages and losses?

Or

Discuss the source of information aftermath of a disaster.

Ans. For assessment to be effective, the process needs to provide an objective view of not only the extent and type of damage but also identify secondary threats like epidemics, resource availability and the local coping capacity. Finally the assessment process should make recommendations to inform and guide the actions, interventions and resources needed to facilitate long-term rehabilitation and development.

Damage assessment is usually conducted at two stages of a disaster:

A preliminary or rapid assessment is conducted immediately after a disaster. It is an initial exercise to guide relief operations. Initial assessment concentrates on immediate life saving and relief measures.

At a later stage, a detailed assessment is conducted for planning and implementing reconstruction programs. It determines specific information related to nature, location, extent of loss, and the resulting needs of the affected people. It helps in determining compensation for repair, retrofitting or reconstruction. The detailed assessment is a multi-sectoral exercise conducted at the end of the emergency phase, depending on the accessibility and status of immediate needs. For example, the post-tsunami assessments report pre pared by the World Bank, ADB and UN system lists the following sectors, housing, health and education, agriculture and livestock, fisheries, livelihoods (micro enterprises and others), rural and municipal infrastructure, transportation, coastal protection and hazard risk management for India.

It is important that the assessment process and tools are "transparent, flexible, adaptable, credible, inclusive and participatory."

The assessment process needs to be planned step-by-step and managed accordingly. The sequence of activities which form a part of the process may be classified as:

- Identification of information needs and sources for reliable data.
- Data collection.
- Data analysis and interpretation.

- Reporting of conclusions, forecast etc to planners and policy makers, who are the end users of the report.

Methodology: Various formats of assessment are used according to the system prevalent where the disaster has occurred. However, recent assessments undertaken are generally based on the standard internationally accepted methodology developed by the United Nations Economic Commission for Latin America and the Caribbean (ECLAC). The assessment format described in the subsequent sections draws from the ECLAC method. This methodology uses a stock and flow analysis that evaluates effect on:

- Physical assets that will have to be repaired, restored, replaced or discounted in the future
- Income flows that will not be realized until the asset is repaired or rebuilt.
- Performance of the economy in terms of the macro-economic aggregates

For case of computation, ECLAC uses the following terms:

(1) Direct damages: are inflicted on immovable assets and on stock which include goods under process, raw materials, spare parts, finished products in stock etc. This category comprises of all the damages that occurred right at the time of disaster. Primarily, it includes the total or partial destruction of buildings, infrastructure (bridges, roads etc), installations (power lines, water supply system) machinery, equipment, means of transportation (rail coaches, buses etc), furniture, damage to farmland (including destruction of crops ready for harvest, irrigation works and the like.

(2) Indirect Losses: refers to the flows or goods and services that will not be provided till the time reconstruction of the asset is completed. The indirect losses result from a direct damage to production capacity and social and economic infrastructure. It also includes increases in the current costs of productions or service. The following components are generally considered for computing indirect losses:

(i) Higher operational costs due to destruction of infrastructure and losses to production and income. For example losses due to unsold perishable items or damaged goods.

(ii) Diminished production or service due to interruptions caused by the calamity.

(iii) Additional costs incurred for reconstruction or starting the production or service afresh.

(iv) Increased costs due to budgetary reorientation.

(v) Income reduction.

(vi) Costs incurred by all parties involved in attending to the affected population to provide emergency relief etc.

(vii) Additional costs related to new situations arising from a disaster like public awareness campaigns to prevent epidemics etc.

(viii) Lost income or production due to the "linkage" effects for example destruction of a factory affects the income of suppliers including ancillary and subsidiary industries.

(ix) Any other side effect like traffic congestion cost, pollution cost etc.

(3) Macroeconomic Effect- reflect the impact of the disaster in the performance of the main economic variables in the affected country. The important macroeconomic effects are those that impact the economic health of the country in terms of Gross Domestic Product, trade balance, indebtedness and public finance, monetary reserves and gross investment. While the magnitude of a disaster determines the time frame for macroeconomic estimates, normally the remainder of the year in which the disaster occurs is considered for "short-term" plus the next one or two years for "medium-term" calculations. Frequently used indicators for estimating the macro-economic effects are:

(i) *Gross Domestic Product (GDP)*- Used to estimate the disaster induced losses at constant prices in the production of goods and services in the recovery period, including the time needed to recoup lost capacity.

(ii) Gross Investment- reflects the suspension or deferral of ongoing development projects due to the disaster. In the following year, however, gross investment will increase as reconstruction activity gets underway.

(iii) Balance of Payments- are affected by disasters in terms of decline in exports, increase in imports for the recovery and reconstruction period, relief donations in cash or kind, reinsurance payments from abroad and reductions in foreign debt servicing options. The estimations is based on the medium and long-term external financing requirement for reconstruction and the external aid or loans required for recovering from the deterioration of monetary reserves.

(iv) Public Finances- refer to the estimation of shortfall in government revenues, increased current spending for relief and rehabilitation and increased current spending for relief and rehabilitation due to the disaster.

(v) Prices and Inflation- refers to the estimation of increased prices due to shortfall of goods and services after a disaster.

(vi) Employment- refers to the overall effects of the employment scenario in all sectors due to destruction of production capacity on the one hand and increased demand for skilled reconstruction personnel on the other.

(4) Sources of Information: In the immediate aftermath of a disaster, most information channels are blocked, so detailed information availability is low. The assessment specialist therefore has to gather information from various sources to reach an objective view of the damage and loss accrued. The primary sources of information are:

(i) *Strategic Sources*- Data collected from a network of social organisations, both national and international, research agencies etc.

(ii) Media Reports- can help in understanding the geographical extent of the disaster, locating data sources and getting an independent analysis of the event

(iii) Maps- essential aid of the details of the affected area

(iv) Reconnaissance Missions- to ensure filling of data gaps and getting a feel of the data requirements

(v) Surveys- field level surveys are important for overall assessment

(vi) Secondary Data Analysis- like population, housing census, age-sex distribution to understand pre-disaster situation and normal trends of growth, employment etc.

(vii) Interpersonal Communications- with professionals and community members if possible

(viii) Remote sensing data- for overall damage scenario.

Q3. How to assess the damages and losses in social sector?

Ans. Damages like human loss, damage to housing and human settlements and loss to sectors like education, health and culture are covered in social sector damage. Though it is generally agreed that the social sector losses are "intangible" like trauma after loss of family and livelihood, lack of motivation etc and cannot be computed, those pertaining to human loss, asset loss and loss to society will always remain significant effects of disasters.

(1) Affected Population: The loss of human lives is the greatest loss that an affected region has to bear and has far-reaching implications on the society. Risk to human lives during a disaster varies according to age, gender, social factor etc. Poverty and social imbalances also contribute to the risk. A quantitative assessment of the size and characteristics of the affected population is the central part of the assessment process. An objective estimation of the affected population is essential for obtaining a correct overview of the disaster and losses in each sector. The humanitarian response is designed according to the needs of the affected population and provides reference point against which all the consistency of other estimates can be benchmarked.

Disaster assessments must begin with demarcation of the affected area, immediately followed by the size and, characteristics of the population affected. The data most often used for such estimates are the recent population and housing census. If recent data is not available, appropriate projections should be made or available data analyzed to determine whether there has been a large influx or decline of population during the inter-census period. Affected population is classified into primary, secondary and tertiary to establish a link between direct damages and indirect losses.

Primary affected population- includes people affected by direct impact of the disaster and consists of the dead, injured and disabled and also those who suffered material losses as a direct and immediate consequence of the disaster. The primary affected people were present in the affected are during the time of the disaster.

Secondary and tertiary affected population- This is the population that suffers from the disaster's indirect effects. The secondary affected population resides within or near the boundaries of the affected area while the tertiary affected population resides far away from the disaster site.

Direct and indirect effects of disasters are reflected in mortality, morbidity, migration etc. While mortality refers to the deaths as a consequence of a disaster, morbidity may arise due to epidemics or infectious diseases in a relief shelter, which may result in some deaths later. The demographic scenario may change due to migration also as loss of land, property or livelihood may lead to population displacement. In addition the data needs to be disaggregated into age-sex categories so that the effects on the elderly, children, women and more vulnerable are not overlooked. A large impact on these groups may extensively modify the prevailing demographic structure of the affected region.

The computation of demographic losses therefore needs to cover not only the dead and injured, but also the diseased, weak and displaced due to a disaster.

(2) Housing and Human Settlements: Housing is often not only a shelter for families but a setting for an economic enterprise as well. Calamities can cause varying degrees of damage depending on various factors like quality of construction, materials used, construction technology, type of dwelling, location etc. Restoration of respectable habitat to the affected population is one of the most crucial activities; it is also important that the reconstructed and restored houses are risk resistant. To ensure risk reduction of vulnerable construction in the post-disaster phase, an assessment of the type and extent of housing damage is required.

The geographic location of the settlement is the first assessment information required to understand its setting with respect to landforms and proximity to natural features like lakes, river etc. It should then describe the typology (urbon or rural), ownership and functional usage of each dwelling unit. Dwelling units that house small or medium scale industries have greater implications on the economy and livelihoods during disasters.

Direct damage in this sector refers to damage or destruction to housing, domestic furniture and equipment, public buildings and urban infrastructure. Damage to buildings is classified as:

- Completely destroyed buildings or those beyond repair.
- Partially destroyed buildings with possibility of repair.
- Unaffected buildings or those with only minor damage.

The basic components of assessment in this sector are based on:

- **Buildings:** The possible damage is to structure and non-structural elements. Structural elements consist of beams, joints, columns, panels, load bearing walls, foundations etc. Non structural elements include partition walls, internal installations, false ceilings, windows, cladding etc. The most severe damage is generally structural in nature and may require complete demolition of the building while non-structural damage is more visible but easy to repair.
- **Furnishings:** refers to furniture, utensils, clothing, domestic appliances and equipment that need to be repaired or replaced.
- **Equipment**: In addition to the usual fittings like sanitary and electrical devices (which are calculated in furnishings), some buildings may have air-conditioning systems, water pumps, elevators, security and recreation systems which get damaged in a disaster.
- **Public buildings-** need to be estimated separately due to the specific functions performed by them and livelihood of employees in each. The housing and human settlements specialist must also estimate damage to public spaces like parks, green zones etc.
- **Other direct damages-** refers to the damages of household connections to public utilities like water and sanitation services, electricity and gas lines.

The indirect losses are estimated on the basis of:

- Cost of reconstruction related demolition and debris removal- where some portions of damaged buildings may have to be demolished before reconstruction. This depends largely on the type of material used for construction

- Cost of reducing vulnerability- in terms of soil stabilisation, strengthening of the building during reconstruction to reduce the risk of damage in the next disaster.
- Relocation costs- if reconstruction on the same site is not possible (due to drainage problems, changing river courses etc), the cost of relocation in terms of cost of land, provision of basic services, titles deeds, transportation of household assets has to be estimated.
- Temporary housing- refers to costs accrued during the period of reconstruction and repair of damaged units.

(3) Education and Culture: This sector assesses the damage to the sector's infrastructure, equipment and general functioning. It is important to ascertain the loss to the education sector, as delay in reconstruction and repair can have far-reaching repercussions and psychological effects among the affected population while resuming the system early has a positive influence on social rehabilitation.

The direct damage refers to destruction and damage to buildings, furniture and equipment and materials, works or volumes of a cultural nature stored in heritage building. Damage assessment would depend on:

(i) Classification of buildings- Buildings are classified according to their functional usage as

(a) Teaching Premises- includes the damage to buildings, laboratories and equipment and recreational spaces within the premise

(b) Cultural Heritage buildings- may be public historic buildings like museums or archaeological sites, state collections of historic value or even private heritage collections that have suffered damage in disasters. As there are no standards for assessment, each building and its collections or equipment has to be assessed individually.

(c) Sports facilities- like gymnasiums, stadiums and other sports facilities damaged in a disaster

The indirect losses in this sector include:

(ii) Damage due to temporary used of educational institutions and cultural premises as relief shelters- Stadium, schools, etc are used as relief shelters and suffer damage as they are not designed to house a large number of people for a long period. The cost of repair of these facilities and equipment therein has to be assessed as indirect losses.

Demolition and removal of debris- Due to the diverse locations and variety of construction materials used, this cost is estimated based on volume of material to be removed and the unit cost of removal or transportation for each establishment.

(iii) Temporary rents and leases- refers to the rent paid due to the establishment running from a different location where repair or reconstruction has taken place.

(iv) Vulnerability reduction- refer to the cost of strengthening or retrofitting the existing building

(v) Relocation- accrues only when the building has to be shifted to a new site

(vi) Loss of income- is the income that will not be received by teachers and staff of the educational or cultural institution while repair or reconstruction is under way.

(4) Health Sector: All disasters have an impact on the health sector, either due to the large number of people dead or injured, damage to the health care network and preventive measures for complex emergencies (epidemics for the affected population. The impact on this sector is both short-term and long-term.

The direct damages include the following:

(i) Health infrastructure like hospitals, health centres, clinics, blood banks, health sector offices which may suffer structural and non-structural damage.

(ii) Furniture and equipment- like medical and surgical equipment, non-medical equipment (computers, air-conditioning), furniture, etc.

The indirect losses include

(i) Demolition and clean up costs- refers to the demolition of unsafe buildings, removal of debris and land improvement.

(ii) Disaster mitigation costs- include the adoption of preventive measures in the structural and non-structural aspects or in organisational-administrative aspects for making the system resilient to future disasters.

(iii) Cost of treating victims- include costs related to additional medical examinations, hospitalisation costs, long-term treatments, expenses for medicines, transportation of patients, cost of overtime of staff etc.

iv) Cost of public health and epidemiological interventions- include the public health interventions necessary for preventing epidemics and other latent diseases. The costs include those of vector control, vaccination campaigns, epidemiological surveillance and food safety.

(v) Increased cost of preferential healthcare for vulnerable groups- costs of special interventions for single mothers, elderly and children under five.

(vi) Additional indirect health operating costs- include the costs of replacement of personnel, strengthening of infrastructure, mobile medical support, public information etc.

(vii) Increased public and private costs owning to higher sickness rates- includes the cost of treatment and additional services to be provided to the sick.

Q4. Highlight the assessment procedure of loss and damage in infrastructure sector.

Ans. Disasters damage infrastructure that provides amenities and services to the people. Basic services like drinking water, electricity, roads etc. if affected not only create difficulties for the community but also pose problems for the relief workers in conducting search, rescue, evacuation etc. A quick assessment of the infrastructure damage would help in the repair and reconstruction process to begin early. Therefore infrastructure sector assessment is crucial in the damage and loss assessment process. In this section, the assessment procedures of energy and water and sanitation are described as examples for other services in the sector.

(1) Energy: As a crucial infrastructure, energy works on a wide network of generation, transmission and distribution facilities. Due to the extensive installations in this sector, the possible damage due to disasters is also immense. Energy sector can be assessed by electrical energy and oil energy. While direct damages to both the sectors refer to the immediate damage to infrastructure and inventories available in a disaster. Indirect losses refer to the costs of meeting the energy demand during the recovery period and loss of profit thereon.

Electrical Sector: Disasters have direct impact on three major components viz. generation units, transmission lines and distribution grids and power distribution centres. The damages are calculated as follows:

(i) **Electricity Generation Plants**- refers to all the facilities attached to hydroelectric, geothermal or conventional power plants driven by steam, gas and gas turbines. The facilities would differ with each type of plant. The assessment should include the cost of repair or installation of equipment and machinery that deliver power to the generator, equipment used for processing of the energy and the building that house all generating equipment.

(ii) **Transmission and Distribution System-** includes transmission, sub-transmission and distribution lines and grids as well all electrical sub-stations used for transmission of power from generation plants to final consumers.

(iii) **Energy Distribution Centres and other Works-** includes electricity measurement and dispatch centres with state-of-the art machinery and equipment and buildings for administrative offices.

Indirect losses in this sector include the additional cost of meeting the interim energy demands during the reconstruction period and also the net income lost to companies during this period. The method of calculation is explained below:

(i) **Temporary Electricity Supply-** The cost incurred for supplying electricity through other means will depend on the time required for rehabilitation, which in turn depends on the magnitude and extent of damage caused by the disaster. This involves estimating the temporary demand for electricity in all sectors (residential, industrial, commercial) and the operating costs on the basis of fuel requirements and cost of delivery through temporary arrangements.

(ii) **Other Indirect Losses-** include profits not received by the electricity utility during the rehabilitation period. This would be the difference between the net income during normal times and the income estimated in the disaster scenario.

Oil Sector: In a disaster, the oil sector sustains damages to its production, refining and distribution facilities. The direct damages in this sector are estimated on the basis of the following:

(i) Production Facilities- refers to structures, equipment and facilities, on-shore or off-shore, used on drill and operate the production wells. They include control rigs, deep drilling rigs, off-shore platforms and the network of pipelines and equipment for production.

(ii) **Oil Refineries-** includes all installations, processing towers, storage facilities and pipelines.

(iii) **Distribution Facilities-** Dedicated facilities for distribution and sale of the final product (gas and oil) and bituminous residues (used in road construction) are included in this sector

(iv) **Other Facilities-** includes the buildings used for administrative purposes.

Like the electricity sector, indirect losses include the additional cost of meeting the requirements for oil and oil derivatives during the rehabilitation period and the profit lost during this time. Specifically, it includes impact on:

(i) **Temporary Supply of and Oil Derivatives**- cost of providing oil products through alternative means

(ii) **Other Indirect Losses-** implies the income loss to the sector during the rehabilitation period.

The damage and loss in these sectors are broken down into domestic and foreign currency for purposes of balances of payments and into public and private sector costs for purposes of national accounting. The energy sector assessment is intrinsically linked to environmental assessment due to incidences of oil spill, release of toxic substances etc.

(2) Drinking Water & Sanitation: One of the most crucial social infrastructures, water and sanitation issues have great epidemiological implications during a disaster. Early restoration of this sector plays a role in avoiding spread of infections and epidemics in a post-disaster scenario and constitutes a public health priority. Assessment of this sector requires a multi-disciplinary and holistic approach among its component elements. This sector consists of three major sub-components viz drinking water supply systems, wastewater disposal systems solid waste collection and disposal systems. A brief overview of the damage and loss assessment is given below:

Direct Damages

(i) Drinking Water Supply Systems:

(a) Damage to infrastructure and equipment (urban and rural) with respect to type of repair or materials required, unit construction prices at replacement value and cost or repairs.

(b) Loss of stocks (chemicals, stored water, spare parts and other assets)

(ii) Wastewater Disposal Systems:

(a) Damage to infrastructure and equipment (urban and rural)

(b) Loss of stock (chemicals, spare parts equipment etc)

(iii) Solid waste disposal systems:

(a) Damage to infrastructure and equipment

(b) Damage to access routes to facilities and dumps

(c) Impact of waste disposal dumps

Indirect Losses

(i) Drinking water Supply Systems:

(a) Rehabilitation activities like distribution through tankers, purchase of equipment, overtime to tanker drivers etc.

(b) Reduction in potable water output due to damage or contamination at source.

(c) Reduction in operational costs due to partial functioning of the system.

(d) Increase in potable water production costs.

(e) Losses due to income not received.

(f) Insurance coverage.

(ii) Wastewater Disposal Systems:

(a) Rehabilitation activities (network inspection, repairs etc).

(b) Reduction in treatment capacity.

(c) Increase in wastewater treatment costs.

(d) Losses due to income not received.

(e) Insurance coverage.

(iii) Solid waste Disposal Systems:

(a) Losses due to income not received.

(b) Decrease in solid waste collection and disposal.

(c) Insurance costs.

Q5. Discuss the assessment procedure of loss and damage for economy and environment.

Ans. Economy and environment are important components of society. While the economy has a direct bearing on the economic well-being and social status of the people, the state of environment affects the overall quality of life. The economic sector primarily consists of agriculture, manufacturing and commerce and service sectors.

(1) Agriculture: Hydro-meteorological disasters like floods, storms, cyclones, droughts etc. affect the agriculture mostly. Hazards of geological origin like earthquakes and landslides have a localized direct impact, but far-reaching indirect impacts like food shortage or damage to storage facilities. The products of the agriculture sector are processed and sold by the commerce sector, so that assessment specialist for agriculture should work closely with that of the latter.

The direct damages to agriculture refer to losses of capital assets. They can be classified as:

(i) Damage/Loss of agricultural fields- refers to the loss of fertility of the field, which may take a long time to recover. This is done by assigning a value to what the land would have produced in 10 years based on its average productivity per hectare.

(ii) Damage to agricultural infrastructure and equipment- refer to infrastructure like irrigation and drainage channels, storage areas, chicken coops, aquaculture pools etc that are damaged or destroyed and farming equipment used.

(iii) Production losses- includes the crops ready to be harvested that were destroyed. If the disaster occurs when the crops were still growing, only losses to labour and inputs need to be accounted for.

(iv) Losses of stock- includes already harvested produce, if any, livestock, stock of seeds or other inputs.

Indirect losses in agriculture sector refer to the losses due to decrease in production through the recovery period and the cost of the mitigation efforts to prevent such damage in future. Estimated time for recovery and re-establishment of production and supply chain are critical factors in assessing the indirect losses. An intrinsic feature of the agriculture sector in developing economies is the "backyard economies" carried out by women as a source of subsistence purposes or for additional income generation. Though run with minimum investment, these activities provide for food needs or many households. The losses in such activities are total in a disaster and recovery is difficult. Related impacts like loss of employment, adverse food and export balances, output and prices are indicators of loss. The following framework can provide an overview of the damages in this sector.

Table : Overview of the damages in agriculture sector

Aspects likely to be damaged	**Agriculture**	**Fisheries**
Source/Assets	• Loss of farmland due to erosion, salinity or sedimentation. • Loss of livestock.	• Rivers, ponds and lakes due to environmental degradation, pollution, changing river courses or any other cause.
Tools, equipment and infrastructure	• Infrastructure and tools such as ploughs, carts, tractors, storage sheds etc. • Damage to irrigation structures like check dams, canals etc.	• Boats and nets • Fisheries and aquaculture infrastructure (fishing ports, cold storages etc).
Inputs and products	• Seeds, fertilizers for subsistence crops and cash crops. • Harvested crops.	• Catch/production of fish, prawns etc.
Access to inputs and resources	• Availability of resources, skills and knowledge for replacement and repairs. • Capacity to procure.	• Availability of resources, skills and knowledge for replacement and repairs. • Capacity to procure.
Employment and Income	• Loss of income due to temporary paralysis of activities. – for both men and women engaged in the economic activity. – for different types of ownership like single farmer, cooperatives, self-help groups etc.	

(2) Environment: While environment is an asset, providing resources like food, water, energy, it also provides services like dilution and transformation of waste, carbon sequestration, maintenance of water cycle etc. While extreme events are a part of the ecosystem process, the interaction between ecosystem and human system result in various environmental changes, which may have adverse impacts on the human society. Damage to environment due to disasters can be direct, through loss of soil cover, deforestation etc or indirect, through increased pollution, habitat or biodiversity loss etc.

Assessment of environmental damage consists of estimating the changes brought about by the disaster to the ecosystem. The following table gives an idea of the range of services provided by various ecosystems.

Table : Range of services provided by various ecosystems

Ecosystem	Goods	Services
Agro-ecosystem	–Food and Fibre crops –Crop genetic resources	–Maintain Watershed functions (infiltration, soil protection,) –Provide habitat for birds, pollinators, soil organisms –Build soil organic matter –Sequester atmospheric carbon
Forest ecosystem	–Fuel wood and Fodder –Timber –Drinking and Irrigation water –Non-Timber Products (honey, herbs etc) –Genetic Resources	–Remove air pollutants –Emit oxygen –Cycle nutrients –Maintain watershed functions (soil stabilization) –Maintain biodiversity –Sequester atmospheric carbon –Moderate weather extremes and impacts –Generate soil –Provide for aesthetic enjoyment and recreation
Freshwater ecosystem	–Drinking and irrigation water –Fish –Hydro-electricity –Genetic Resources	–Buffer water flow (control timing and volume) –Dilute and carry away wastes

		–Cycle nutrients –Maintain biodiversity –Provide aquatic habitat –Provide transportation corridor –Provide for aesthetic enjoyment and recreation
Grassland ecosystems	–Livestock (meat, leather etc) –Water for human consumption and irrigation –Genetic resources	–Maintain array of watershed functions –Cycle nutrients –Remove air pollutants and emit oxygen –Maintain biodiversity –Sequester atmospheric carbon –Generate soil –Provide for aesthetic enjoyment and recreation
Coastal ecosystem	–Fish and shellfish –Fishmeal –Sea-weeds (for food and industrial use) –Genetic resources	–Moderate storm impacts –Provide wildlife habitat –Maintain biodiversity –Dilute wastes –Provide harbours and transportation routes –Provide for aesthetic enjoyment and recreation

In post-disaster assessment, the changes in the goods and services need to be checked. The apparent changes should be assessed in terms of:

(i) Unusual landform/geomorphic changes- may occur after earthquakes, landslides, volcanic eruptions.

(ii) Changes in natural drainage- caused due to changes in river courses or drainage systems which may have a long-term impact on the ground and surface water reserves.

(iii) Soil degradation- soil erosion after floods, salinity after tsunami or seawater ingress or silting can lead to long-term impacts on the productivity, which in turn affects the farming community. Impacts on common property resources like grazing land affects the livestock and related sectors.

(iv) Destruction of trees- Disasters like cyclones, tsunamis, floods etc cause large-scale destruction of tree cover, affecting the community. There is need to know the species, number and location of such damage.

(v) Water contamination- contamination of water bodies and sources have serious implications on the health of the affected community

(vi) Loss of unique plant/animal species and their habitat- Loss of habitat due to a disaster can result in loss of biodiversity.

The environmental damages have to be assessed in a participatory manner so that the local knowledge, context and dependencies with relation to the environment are incorporated without any bias.

Q6. How to assess damage to women and vulnerable groups? Discuss.

Ans. Natural disasters do not affect people equally. In fact, a vulnerability approach to disasters would suggest that inequalities in exposure and sensitivity to risk as well as inequalities in access to resources, capabilities, and opportunities systematically disadvantage certain groups of people, rendering them more vulnerable to the impact of natural disasters. Disasters often have a differential impact on women primarily due to the socially sanctioned gender stereotyping, which identify them as victims. It is increasingly accepted that development would not be sustainable unless more vulnerable groups like women, children, aged etc are incorporated into the system and their special needs met. It is also accepted that the needs of these more vulnerable groups have to be incorporated within each sector of assessment, rather than a separate assessment format. For example, the housing and settlement sector needs to take into account the needs of these vulnerable groups within its framework. This should be encouraged to build capacity of the most vulnerable groups, favour gender equity and empower the marginalised.

Though women are looked upon as care-givers and their activities unpaid and given a much lower status than men, they contribute to the household income through a variety of "backyard" or informal sector activities. As a consequence of disasters, the women face complete destruction of their activities. Not only do they face direct damages like loss of house or means of production, they also sustain high opportunity costs because they lose income because of the time spent in emergency related activities and increased amount of unpaid reproductive work.

The impact of disasters on women can be assessed through the following:

- **Activity profile-** Changes in activities post-disaster for e.g., time taken for collection of water or firewood.
- **Access and control profile-** refers to access to resources and opportunities like education, income etc. This analysis helps identification of the impediments for equitable participation.
- **Analysis of influencing factors-** Changes in family headship, family income etc have a bearing on the socio-economic status of women and their coping capacities. For example both the access and control profile and activity profile may change with a women becoming the head of the household.
- **Needs and priorities-** On the basis of the analysis the specific needs of women should be incorporated in the rehabilitation mechanism.

Q7. Why disaster recovery planning is called a unique Windows of Opportunity? Explain the factors affecting recovery.

Or

What are the various factors affecting recovery?

Ans. In a sense, the aftermath of a disaster can provide a unique window of opportunity to assess the socio-economic vulnerabilities that contributed to the disaster in a society. For instance, disaster experience gives opportunities to identify fault lines in the development policies: the mistakes of past development policies and strategies, which resulted in increased risks. The disaster experience may also helps to develop a new awareness of risk. It may facilitate generation of a new knowledge, which is in turn expected to bring various stakeholders together around a shared awareness of the nature of risk. In addition, disaster recovery is a phase which expose institutional weaknesses: the corruption, lack of human resources and weak institutional structures that allowed high risk planning land use and discouraged appropriate monitoring before the disaster have been exposed. In a nut shell, it can be said that critical decisions, that previously unaddressed, can no longer be ignored and choice must be made during disaster recovery planning.

It is observed that most often there is a period- window of opportunity- to incorporate a planning framework into the disaster recovery effort. It is also an ideal time to raise awareness and to re-examine socio-economic vulnerability patterns and to plan for the future disasters.

Total recovery from a disaster is measured in four ways: (1) emotional recovery of the victims; (2) economic recovery, including replacement of the income lost, the restoration of jobs and/or the means of production, and restoration of the markets; (3) replacement of physical losses, which includes replacement of personal belongings, the home, and in some cases, the replacement of land; and (4) replacement of opportunity. In order to develop appropriate responses to shorten recovery time, it is necessary to understand what factors can affect time of recovery and the different effect of different strategies.

Factors Affecting Recovery: There are many factors that control the amount of time between the disaster and a return to normal.

(1) Risk of secondary disasters: Many hazards are accompanied by second events. For example, an earthquake can be followed by a series of secondary tremors. These may last for only a few days or for as long as several months. Some tremors may even be stronger than the original earthquake. Survivors may be reluctant to begin reconstruction or even salvage materials from the rubble until the threat of a secondary disaster has passed.

(2) Uncertainty regarding possible relocation: Most often, the victims are uncertain as to whether or not they can safely remain at their previous home site or at the place they had moved to after the disaster. They will hesitate to engage in long-term activities. Uncertainty about relocation can be caused both by a reluctance to occupy a site that was vulnerable in the disaster and by uncertainty about government intentions regarding relocation or resettlement.

(3) Delayed materials: The speed with which recovery begins depends on the availability of tools and materials. In almost every disaster, there are adequate resources for rebuilding either in the community or in the surrounding region. Access to these materials, however, may be reduced by official actions, such as evacuation. In those cases where materials are not available, reconstruction will be delayed pending arrival of adequate supply the necessary materials.

(4) Expert advice: One of the major problems following a disaster whose advice to follow. At all levels of the disaster-affected community- from the government's relief officials to the field directors or voluntary agencies, down to the local inhabitants themselves- people are constantly bombarded with information, much of it conflicting. Persons at all levels of the disaster relief system, and especially those with no previous disaster training or experience, are constantly faced with the dilemma of interpreting the information and deciding on its relevance to their situation. This advice may not be suited to the local situation: it could be too highly technical; it may not be cost-effective; or it may not be culturally acceptable. Often the people offering the advice are not qualified to give it. Motivated but inexperienced volunteers provide most of the labor for relief operations. While the advice they give is often based on the best of intentions, it usually comes from preconceived ideas as to what a relief operation should be, not from training or experience. Thus conflicts of opinion are bound to arise. The problem of conflicting expertise and advice can be overcome only through adequate pre-disaster planning and training of relief personnel at all decision-making levels within the relief structure.

(5) Inflation and market instability: In situations where material is available, recovery time is influenced by its cost. If prices are not controlled and high inflation occurs, recovery time will increase. Similarly, an unstable market affected by speculation or hoarding will prolong reconstruction, as will excessive customs delays in cases where building materials must be imported. To be effective, prices must be controlled in all parts of the market.

(6) Land tenure problems: Politically sensitive and among the most difficult factors to address are land ownership, land distribution, and legal land reform. After a disaster, these issues are often further complicated by such questions as: Should victims be assisted to rebuild on land that is not their own? Where landless people should be resettled? Who will provide the land?

(7) Public rejection of Plans: Often in the rush to provide assistance, agencies will undertake programs without considering their acceptability to the victims. There are numerous examples of victims rejecting aid offered by interveners, both governmental and non-governmental. The reason may be that the aid is culturally unacceptable or unaffordable.

Whatever the reasons, time and effort, again. The time lost is an extension or recovery time.

(8) Surveys: While surveys can be valuable aids it planning emergency or reconstruction actions, if they are properly planned and develop relevant information. However, in some cases, actions have been delayed until surveys are completed. The problem is not that surveys are not needed, but rather the type of data that is most appropriate and the method that should be used to obtain it. The loss of this time can mean loss of resources and commitment that would be invaluable in reconstruction.

(9) Irrelevant aid: The arrival of massive amounts of useless relief goods, untrained personnel and volunteers, and untrained officials all add second strategy, but it does require an understanding of disasters. Typical actions are provision of building materials for use in temporary shelters that can later be incorporated into permanent housing; the normal economic systems; and setting up work programs for victims that not only provide resources but also accomplish reconstruction objectives.

(10) Bureaucracy: Disaster response requires a streamlined decision-making process, flexible standard operating procedures, and good internal communications.

In short, to accelerate the recovery process, agencies must provide or restore the infrastructures of a community, provide the materials required, and make opportunities for the victims.

Q8. What are the important features of a disaster recovery plan? Discuss the pre and post disaster recovery planning process.

Or

Write down the pre and post disaster recovery planning process.

Ans. An ideal disaster recovery plan will have following features:

(1) Clarity of policy and direction: One of the most important tasks for those in positions of authority is to provide a clear picture of goals and objectives; the means by which they are to be attained, and the "rules" that govern post-disaster actions. On the basis of these policies and standards, relief and reconstruction assistance can be provided in an equitable manner and delays resulting from indecision can be reduced. Such policies and directions are best developed before a disaster.

(2) Leadership: Leadership is obviously an important factor in the response to a disaster. Choosing the right leadership for the task force itself will vary with the circumstances and may depend heavily on personal characteristics of potential candidates for this role. Because a disaster often involves a good deal of reliance on outside assistance, a clear choice of leadership for managing long-term recovery and reconstruction also provides a central point of contact, information, and accountability for the outside world. This, in turn, increases the community's ability to marshal the external resources its needs.

(3) Guidelines for communication: There is a need for good communications during all phases of a disaster. The emphasis, however, should not be on improving the means of communication (that is, radios and other electronic communications equipment), but on improving the flow of information and the type of information communicated. Good communication is the art of knowing what type of information to send; how to prepare it in such a way that it is relevant to the needs of those receiving it; and communicating with the right people.

(4) Technical accuracy: The plan for post-disaster recovery and reconstruction must tap broad combination of resources and expertise in order to reflect the complex realities. In any post-disaster program, there are always questions that need to be answered by competent technical personnel. This information must be available and presented in such a way that it will be comprehensible to those who are working at each level of the program. Formation of an interdisciplinary reconstruction planning task force is the best way to guide the process of constructing the plan. Organizing appropriate representation on the task force is as important aspect of interdisciplinary planning effort.

(5) Sources of Resource mobilisation: Post-disaster programs are dependent upon an adequate flow of cash. Because the costs of purchasing materials on a large scale will be fairly high, and financial institutions are themselves likely to be disrupted, agencies may experience difficulty arranging credit, and many items or services will have to be purchased with cash: Agencies can anticipate these problems and develop mechanisms to avoid lengthy delays.

Pre-disaster recovery planning process: A common misconception of recovery is that it begins when the disaster response ends. Long term recovery starts on Day 1 post-disaster; however, it is true that governments often focuses on response operations, and on stabilizing the situation, can often times be overwhelmed by the enormity and complexity of the recovery challenges at hand.

The starting point of the planning process must be an identification of the hazards facing the community and the risks they pose to life and property. Hazard identification and risk assessment can said to be the cornerstones of mitigation. Before discussing the process, some key terms needs to be discussed. These are hazard identification, vulnerability assessment, and risk assessment. The term hazard identification refers to the process of "defining and describing a hazard, including its physical characteristics, magnitude and severity, probability and frequency, causative factors, and locations/areas affected." "Assessing vulnerability" means taking stock of the degree to which human life and property are exposed to damage from that hazard; in other words, how much damage and loss of life could the community conceivably suffer? This is differentiated from risk assessment, which focuses on probabilities and is described as a process for "evaluating risk associated with a specific hazard and defined in terms of probability and frequency of occurrence, magnitude and severity, exposure, and consequences."

Hazard Identification and Risk Assessment: The first step in hazard identification and risk assessment involves mapping the known natural hazards, a procedure that will vary with the nature of the disaster. Regardless of these variances, the first step is to document all of them and identify as accurately as possible the areas potentially affected by them.

The second step in hazard identification and risk assessment is to develop an inventory, to the extent possible, of the build environment that potentially would be affected by these hazards. This inventory not only will indicate the extent of possible damage from the hazard but will also serve as a rough indicator of the threat to human life because people tend to be where transportation of buildings are, and the total or partial collapse of structures of structures or parts of structures is a primary cause of death and injury in a disaster. This potential damage to life and property is what constitutes vulnerability, and the likelihood of that damage-quantifying the probabilities-is what constitutes risk. A flood in an unpopulated and unbuilt area, for example, poses little or no risk. On the other hand, the risk posed by even a modest earthquake in a metropolitan city can be quite high.

Because predicting the future is strictly a matter of probabilities, the only certain data come from past experience. Thus, planners documenting risk must include in their reports the history of previous natural hazards events, their magnitudes, and an inventory of the human and property damages that occurred. Those magnitudes should be expressed numerically, in a statistical or other mathematical measure, such as the Richter scale (earthquakes), Saffir-Simpson scale (hurricanes), Fujita scale (tornadoes), or flood probabilities (for example, an x-year flood). It is important to build into the process, preferably with the use of computerized databases and Geographical Information System (GIS), a pre-disaster inventory of vulnerable structures and to use this information to evaluate building performance on a geographic basis.

Developing Community Consensus on Disaster Recovery Planning: Developing community consensus is an important aspect of recovery planning. A plan for post-disaster recovery and reconstruction is unlikely to succeed unless it enjoys broad and knowledgeable support both from the public and the government. The challenging question is how to build and maintain that consensus and support. The process of building consensus has two stages. The first involves building consensus around the very need for a plan in the first place. Planners will likely find a need to build public acceptance of the value of planning for post-disaster reconstruction, particularly where the risk is perceived as distant or infrequent. Gaining acceptance of the need to address natural hazards serves as the prelude to the second stage, that of developing a plan and building consensus around its goals and policies. At this point, the planning process is accepted, and the debate is over the specific goals that will emerge and the means of realizing them.

In addition, the recovery plan should contain reasonably extensive and effective opportunities for public input and comment before it is adopted, and those opportunities should allow for meaningful public education in the bargain. Because the plan will need both to be updated periodically and to undergo revisions in the aftermath of actual disasters, it is important to include provisions for ensuring continued public education and input on the plan's goals and purposes.

Institutionalizing Recovery Planning: Some of the important questions that need to be considered during the recovering planning are who will coordinate the process and oversee compliance with the intent of the post-disaster plan? There is no single answer to this question, but there are several possibilities that have worked or can work, depending on local traditions, local government structure, and other factors that may influence this decision such as the nature of the jurisdiction.

Developing a set of guidelines/operational policy is another important aspect in the process of institutionlisation of recovery planning. It involves establishing a line of reporting and designating responsibility for implementing recovery and reconstruction. The process of disaster recovery will proceed more smoothly if a post-disaster plan already has established the mechanisms and timelines for various agency representatives to perform their tasks and to report to the lead agency in order to keep the recovery process well-coordinated.

Evaluating and Updating the Post-disaster Plan: One final issue must be considered in completing the inventory of post-disaster plan elements-that of keeping it current. Plans that age without periodic revision become largely irrelevant, but it is not hard to build into a plan provisions for revisiting the issues addressed and updating the elements in light of new experience. Including a program for periodic review and revision also allows a community to measure its progress and ensure implementation of those actions it decided to address in the pre-disaster period. With the widespread and growing use of various types of community and sustainable development indicators, planners have the opportunity to use this process in the post-disaster plan to incorporate into those indicators measurements of the community's progress toward a more disaster-resistant future.

It does little good to learn valuable new lessons about natural hazards affecting the community if none of them are put to use. It is essential to prepare in the post-disaster plan a means for incorporating those lessons as rapidly as possible into the development regulations that will guide the reconstruction process. This may be, however, one of the most challenging elements of the entire plan precisely because it takes time to study, identify, and analyze new hazards information from a disaster, and even more time to craft regulation in response to them. It is often not possible for all rebuilding to await such analysis. But the plan should contain policy statements indicating clearly, before the disaster occurs, that the most hazardous areas will not necessarily be rebuilt. While it is likely to be impossible to apply these lessons to all post-disaster reconstruction, it is better to apply it where possible than not at all. Providing for some process of review and revision that will allow this to happen is an astute move for any local government.

Post-disaster recovery process: No community can reasonably ratchet up the size of its staff or its stockpile of equipment to meet all the contingencies that might occur in disaster. The sensible approach is to identify these potential shortcomings and remedy them through mutual aids that allow the community to call upon outside resources when they are needed. The post-disaster plan offers an opportunity for community self-assessment to determine where potential deficiencies in resources and personnel might surface following a disaster. The post recovery planning process involves following aspects:

- **Temporary shelter**: Providing the temporary shelter to victims is a part and a function of emergency response, but recovery planners should play a vital role by identifying appropriate sites in advance. Emergency shelter sites generally revert to their original uses, such as schools and community centers, after the recovery period, but other forms of temporary housing, including manufactured housing, can and often do become more permanent than may have originally been envisioned. Planners can help to ensure during the pre-disaster period that, if this happens, the sites identified for such housing are zoned appropriately.
- **Assessment of building conditions and overall damages:** The Preliminary Damage Assessment (PDA) is an ongoing task that may take different forms at different stages of response and recovery, starting with a minimal survey, involving observations from passing vehicles by, police, and emergency management personnel, to more detailed and in-person surveys by building inspectors. The function of damage assessment should be included and addressed as an element in a post-disaster plan regardless of the magnitude of the disaster as a matter of clarifying lines of responsibility.
- **Restoration of utility services**: Restoring utility services is an essential prerequisite for beginning economic recovery and for restoring some measure of comfort to those whose routines have been disrupted. It is a matter of public safety, as well, for

local firefighting ability is at stake when electrically operated water pumps no longer work. It can also be a matter of life and death for home-bound elderly people, the disabled, and other.

- **Establishment of reconstruction priorities**: Public facilities often suffer as much damage as private property in a disaster. Civic buildings, fire and police stations, hospitals, and schools have all suffered damage of destruction in major disasters. One critical function of a post-disaster plan is to establish the community's priorities concerning reconstruction of these facilities, given the obvious fact that limited resources and personnel may not allow simultaneous rebuilding of everything.
- **Financial assistance**: Knowing where to access financial assistance both for restoration of business activity and for residential reconstruction allows for a more smoothly functioning process of recovery and reconstruction. This is the primary reason why the effective use of disaster assistance was identified as a policy objective of the plan. People are deeply concerned about money in the recovery period following a disaster.
- **Re-occupancy standard and permitting**: Post-disaster condition can pose a bewildering variety of threats to public health and safety, many of them lurking in residential buildings and in workplaces. The safety of residential buildings is particularly crucial because of their round-the-clock occupancy. When and under what conditions may people reoccupy partially damaged structures? Clearly, the goal is to rehouse people as soon as this can be done safely. The plan needs to establish how the work involved in performing this task can be done expeditiously and the standards that will be applied for interim reoccupancy of damaged structures. These policies need to be established in the pre-disaster period, though the implementation will flow out of the information generated through the damage assessment process.
- **Land Use planning**: Of the various categories of elements in the post-disaster plan, this section is the most crucial. The

overall intent is to provide for the means of learning valuable new land-use lessons from the disaster, to enable the disaster prone areas to incorporate them consistently into its mitigation plans and to amend its post-disaster plan as needed, and thus to minimize future risk by fostering a culture of adaptation to new information. This is, in other words, the primary feedback loop. More specifically, the appropriate amendments would tend to focus on updating priorities for changes in land uses of properties for acquisition or various forms of hazard mitigation.

- **Replanning of stricken areas**: Replanning uses the new lessons about local hazards to reshape the community's long-term vision. This function ought to be addressed in two stages: pre-disaster and post-disaster. The pre-disaster portion of this element would entail the identification of areas that may not be rebuilt after a disaster, accompanied by options for how those areas may be treated during the post-disaster period. The post-disaster aspect would consist of a review and analysis of these same areas to determine the most appropriate resolution of the planning problems they present.
- **Coordination with non-profit relief services**: The first step in direction is to establish an effective inventory of those non-profit entities that are likely to respond to or be involved with the community in the event of a disaster. For the most part, planners will not deal directly with such services unless they are involved with long-term reconstruction. It is nonetheless valuable to be aware of their role and the external resources they may bring to the community.
- **Transportation:** Disaster victims suffer disconnection with the outside world almost entirely in one of two ways: loss of communications and loss of transportation. Disruption of the latter can take a wide variety of forms, as all modes are vulnerable depending on the circumstances. A thorough plan for regional coordination of the restoration of transportation access needs to consider air, water, rail, and street and highway issues.

- **Coordinated media contact for accuracy and consistency**: Natural disasters offer wonderful opportunities for officials at all levels to garner media attention. The cacophony that is sure to result when everyone is allowed to do so is best avoided with a clear plan of action for directing media questions to a single designated source through whom information from other participants can be channeled. Officials drafting post-disaster plans should anticipate different levels of emergencies and consider what might be appropriate based on the geographic extent and magnitude of the disaster. In disaster field offices, both federal and state media representative are often co-located to facilitate such coordination.

Q9. Explain the concept of disaster management cycle.

Or

Describe the pr and post disaster management system.

Ans. Disaster Management can be defined as the organization and management of resources and responsibilities for dealing with all humanitarian aspects of emergencies, in particular preparedness, response and recovery in order to lessen the impact of disasters.

The disaster management cycle (DMC) illustrates the ongoing process by which governments, businesses, and civil society plan for and reduce the impact of disasters, react during and immediately following a disaster, and take steps to recover after a disaster has occurred. Appropriate actions at all points in the cycle lead to greater preparedness, better warnings, reduced vulnerability or the prevention of disasters during the next iteration of the cycle. The complete disaster management cycle includes the shaping of public policies and plans that either modify the causes of disasters or mitigate their effects on people, property, and infrastructure.

Goals of Disaster Management:

(1) Reduce, or avoid, losses from hazards;

(2) Assure prompt assistance to victims;

(3) Achieve rapid and effective recovery.

The Disaster Management Cycle can be divided into three stages, that is, Pre-disaster, During-disaster and Post-disaster.

- **Pre-disaster:** Preparedness, Prevention and Mitigation are the major activities in pre-disaster stage. It is based upon the principle that prevention is better than cure. In this stage, various preventive measures and activities are undertaken well in advance so as to respond to disasters in an effective way. Much of the disastrous effects could be avoided, if we are well equipped with preparedness, prevention and mitigation measures and give serious attention to the early warnings. Pre-disaster activities should, thus, concentrate on creating disaster resilient structures and communities. For example, in India, cyclones are a common phenomenon that occurs and warnings are generally given beforehand. If preparatory activities can be undertaken well in advance, then it becomes easy to prevent huge losses in terms of lives and property, in the aftermath phase.

- **During-disaster:** Response and Relief are the important activities in the during-disaster stage. It will start in the aftermath of a disaster. It includes immediate activities like search, rescue and evacuation, identification of and management of dead bodies and debris management, provision of first-aid, food, water, shelter, safety and security, health care and sanitation, restoration of basic facilities, etc. For example, when the Indian Ocean Tsunami struck in 2004, one can reflect that all these measures were undertaken immediately.
- **Post-disaster:** The major activities in the post-disaster phase include: Rehabilitation, Reconstruction and Recovery. These activities will ensure that the disaster affected community becomes resilient and return back to normalcy. Generally, this phase takes a long time, as the efforts are made to restore all essential facilities to pre-disaster status. The major focus of this phase is on the measures that could pave way for long-term recovery of social, economic and physical structures, as well as processes in such a way that future disasters are unable to impact severely and irreversibly.

Q10. Describe the various components of recovery.

Ans. It is very difficult to draw a line between the different stages of response and recovery. However, the two stages have very distinctive characteristics. The recovery is comprised of rehabilitation and reconstruction of disaster affected community and area. The precise time when response ends and recovery starts, depends on various factors like disaster type, the extent of damage, level of preparedness, coping capacity of the affected community, the legislative and administrative powers to recover from such situations and political stability and resolve to recover from such situations etc.

After the disaster, the recovery process starts immediately. The affected community starts recovering from the damage and losses incurred due to the impact of disaster. However, the entire process of post-disaster recovery process can broadly be divided into three major parts as described in the below table:

Table : Components of the Recovery Process

Components	Time Line	Activities to be taken care
Short term recovery (Response)	Up to one month	• Damages, loss and need assessment • Support for food, cloths and emergency health • Temporary shelters • Restoration of infrastructure
Medium term recovery (Rehabilitation)	Up to one year	• Intermediate shelters • Continued support for food, cloths and health • Establishment of institutional mechanism • Mobilization of resources • Socio-psycho care • Opening of schools etc.
Long term recovery (Reconstruction)	Several years	• Restoration of permanent housing • Restoration of physical and social infrastructure • Documentation of lessons learnt

In short-term recovery which is called response phase, not much emphasis is given to the physical recovery process.

Physical recovery process is covered in the medium-term and long-term recovery. The medium-term recovery process refers to key activities which facilitates transition from response to recovery. The long-term recovery activities include socio-economic rehabilitation, reconstruction of housing, infrastructure and business etc. Another way of classifying the recovery process is as discussed in the following paragraphs:

Rehabilitation or medium term recovery refers to the actions taken in the aftermath of a disaster to restore basic services and life supporting activities to bring pattern of life to that level as it was existed before the disaster. Based on the activities rehabilitation or short term recovery process can be further classified as following:

(1) Physical Rehabilitation- the restoration of all physical assets and infrastructure like housing, electricity supply, water supply, sewerage, roads and bridges, irrigation networks, communication networks etc.

(2) Social Rehabilitation- the restoration of medical health and education activities in the affected areas as well as the psycho-social care, trauma counseling do take place under this category. Various social welfare schemes for women and children of the affected areas are also taken care under this category.

(3) Economic Rehabilitation- aims to bring the affected community into the mainstream again. Various programmes and activities taken up at this stage are focused towards development of livelihood activities of agricultural farmers, labourers, artisans etc. At this stage special programme to provide immediate employment to the affected community are generally started; if the situation warrants specialized training programmes for generating livelihood options may be started. Few activities like social forestry and food for work programme etc. are usually taken up at this stage.

(4) Other Related Programmes and Activities- programmes and activities under this category include remaining welfare schemes. Few important activities like rehabilitation of environment, debris recycling and management, repair and restoration of monuments are few of the prominent activities taken up here.

Reconstruction is the stage where all programmes and activities taken up at rehabilitation stage are provided with the permanency. Thus, the reconstruction is the stage where long-term development plans are taken up which takes care for future disaster risks and possibilities to reduce such risks by incorporating appropriate measures. The main motive here is to build back better to counter the possibilities of future disasters.

Q11. Elaborate the metamorphosis of housing recovery after major disaster.

Or

Describe the transition of housing recovery after major disaster.

Ans. There are three basic components to household recovery. These are housing recovery, economic recovery, and psychological recovery. All three of these components require resources to recover, but households must invest time to obtain these resources. This includes time to find and purchase alternate shelter, clothing, food, furniture, and appliances to support daily living.

Households typically use three types of housing recovery following a disaster. The first type, *emergency shelter*, consists of unplanned and spontaneously sought locations that are intended only to provide protection from the elements, typically open yards and cars after earthquakes. The second type is *temporary shelter*/temporary housing which includes food preparation and sleeping facilities that usually are sought from friends and relatives or are found in commercial lodging, although mass care facilities in school gymnasiums or church auditoriums are acceptable as a last resort. The temporary housing allows victims to reestablish household routines in non-preferred locations or structures. The last type is *permanent housing*, which reestablishes household routines in preferred locations and structures. There is no single pattern of progression through the stages of housing because households vary in number and sequence of movements and the duration of their stays in each type of housing.

The various stages of transitional housing are tabulated below:

Table : Stages of Transitional Housing

Housing stage	**Time line**	**Description**
Emergency shelters	First few days to weeks	Immediate shelters are the places where an affected community find place to live immediately after a disaster like school, tents etc. Generally limited amenities are provided in such shelters. However, limited provisions for food, water and sanitation are made. Here, people live together with no privacy. Cooked food is supplied to all the residents.

		Generally, there is no provision for independent spaces and entire community stays together. Depending on local conditions and type of disaster, people may be required to stay in such shelters from few days to few weeks before either they return to their homes or shift to temporary shelters. The emergency shelters have environmental considerations similar to crowded places. Such situations require adequate provision for hygienic conditions by providing safe food and drinking water, adequate sanitation, ventilation within the camps and appropriate lighting arrangement etc.; in such conditions one of the major concerns is to control of epidemic outbreak. Such facilities must provide sufficient protection against natural elements like rain, wind, heat and cold etc.
Temporary Shelters and/or Temporary Housing	First few weeks to years	Temporary or intermediate shelters are those places where people have to stay after emergency period is over and till the time they are provided with adequate permanent houses under reconstruction phase. It is an improved version of the earlier stage. Every family gets an independent space for living with proper demarcation of spaces for cooking, bathroom, and sleeping. Here, disaster affected people may be staying in such shelters for longer durations (may be in years). At this stage efforts are made to provide an independent space to every family or to a group of families. These shelters are semi-permanent in nature with a provision of bare

		minimum facilities required for living. Structure should be erected in such a fashion that they can withstand the vagaries of nature in the immediate future. Like in case of earthquake disaster affected areas, there are always chances of aftershocks, so such houses should be able to withstand these shocks. Similarly, the houses should have appropriate provisions to take care of security against natural effects like rain, extreme heat and cold conditions. Adequate light and ventilation arrangements for all houses must be ensured. The semi-permanent/permanent provisions for safe drinking water and adequate sanitation etc. are a must. Under this stage people have to be provided with semi permanent type of bathroom/toilets, kitchen with adequate arrangements for sewerage discharge.
Permanent Housing	Several years	Permanent houses are provided to the affected community after completion of reconstruction phase. These houses have necessary facilities and appropriate environment for a decent comfortable living. Planning the village/site layouts and individual dwelling units require a lot of consideration to accommodate traditional living styles and local cultural values. Use of building material and construction practices also required to be carefully selected, because traditional building material and techniques have been evolved based on the local climatic conditions and availability of good building materials. New building material

		and construction technology may not be fully accepted by the locals. Site selection for new location of the affected village requires not only appropriate soil investigation but also other socio-economic-environmental considerations, based on the local hazard profile. If the reconstruction has to be made on new site, the land acquisition from agriculture and forest land is required, which have its own implications. A careful process and consultations have to be followed with the affected/beneficiaries. Similarly, distance from newly established village/site/location from the exiting site/village require careful examination, which may develop further complications. Proper debris disposal/management, if the construction has to be made on the same site. A proper strategy need to be evolved about the reuse of the debris so generated (especially in case of an earthquake).

Q12. Elucidate the various principles and approaches for post disaster recovery.

Or

What are the various principles of post disaster recovery?

Or

State the approaches of post disaster recovery.

Ans. There are basic principles, which need to be looked into before implementing the recovery programmes. Few of such principles to be followed are:

- Empowerment of local community to take care of recovery process. It is always desirable to have local community involved in the recovery process as it requires local resources.

- Involvement of local community and give them the ownership of the recovery programme
- Give due consideration to the local traditional values, customs with preference to the local material. Priority of the local community shall form the basis for development
- Incorporate disaster risk mitigation components into the recovery process. As discussed in the earlier section, without disaster mitigation efforts, the recovery process may fail in next disasters. Similarly, adopt a holistic and comprehensive multi-hazard approach taking into consideration all possible hazards, which are prevailing at local level as well take care of linkages with the pre-disaster management.
- To achieve these planning principles, one has to have a strong dedicated leadership at all levels including grass roots leaderships.

Disaster events especially big earthquakes have potential of converting a bustling habitat/city/town into ruins. There are several big earthquakes in the recent past at international level, which had caused huge devastations. Majority of such earthquakes disasters had resulted in massive to big recovery programmes. In recovering the earthquake affected areas from disaster situation various models and approaches had been used for effective post-disaster recovery process. Some of the models prevalent at international level include the owner-driven approach, the subsidiary housing approach, the participatory housing approach, the contractor- driven approach in-situ, and the contractor-driven approach ex nihilo. Table 5 indicates the damages caused and recovery strategy adopted for recovering the earthquake affected areas from few of these earthquakes.

It has been observed that two major approaches had been used for recovery of disaster affected areas in India. The approaches can be summarized as following:

- Redevelopment approach is where state governments had played a very effective role in physical recovery and economic rehabilitation of affected areas. In such cases the government procures funding from agencies like World Bank, Asian Development Bank or similar national or international agency for recovery of the disaster affected area. Such approaches are very effective in case of large scale disasters. Similar approach had been very effectively utilized in case of Latur earthquake (Maharashra, 1993) and Bhuj earthquake (Gujarat, 2001) as well as several reconstruction programmes in Andhra Pradesh during the decade of 90's. One of the major highlight of this approach is that a major portion of resources is generally spent on housing and physical infrastructure. As the external agencies are involved with clear guidelines to incorporate mitigation efforts, such recovery programmes result in disaster safe infrastructure and housing.

- Limited intervention approach is where assistance given to affected households with limited or no controls over its use. Here affected families are provided limited assistance and supervision to recover from the disaster. In certain cases the assistance given to affected households with checks and counter-checks for utilisation of funds as per programme guidelines has also been observed. NGO driven community participation with checks and counter-checks for utilisation of funds as per programme guidelines. Community participation to be facilitated in the design of dwellings/settlements, monitoring of quality of construction and procuring of various documents required for establishing entitlements of land.

Q13. Analyse the ***inter linkages between*** **disaster** ***recovery and development.***

Or

What is the relationship between physical recovery and development?

Ans. The 'oughts' and 'shoulds' in disaster recovery planning make for a good reading, but in reality we do not even have anything that can be remotely referred to as a disaster recovery plan. There is no systematic disaster management plan at the central, state and local levels. We all know by now that the real solutions to the problems of rehabilitation and reconstruction lie in the establishment of inter-linkages between disasters and development.

The relationship between disasters and development is, however, not that of straight cause and effect. There are many intricacies in its backward and forward linkages and the underlying network of relationships.

Disasters can seriously degrade a country's long-term potential for sustained development and cause governments to substantially modify their economic and social priorities, as well as developmental programmes. Disasters often force the otherwise stable, sedentary population to move away from their established places of work, and creates psychological stress leading to many dysfunctional consequences. Yet, they do highlight high-risk areas where action must be taken before another disaster strikes.

In the present context, disasters can no longer be viewed as random occurrences caused by nature's wrath. The distinction between natural and man-made disasters is getting blurred with time. The frequency and intensity of disasters have recorded an all time high, as the harmonious balance between human beings and nature has been disturbed to almost irreparable proportions. Faulty urbanisation, population explosion, civil strife, unbalanced industrial growth are the reasons attributed to environmental degradation characterised by global warming, deforestation, desertification, soil erosion and so on. Environmental degradation and mismanagement may aggravate the frequency, severity and predictability of hazards. It could be behind the increased instances of disasters. Disaster management has to thus be placed in the context of the development challenges that the country faces as a whole. There is a significant relationship in the way that disasters and development affect one another.

While disasters are catastrophic events, lessons learnt and incorporated into long-term development planning may serve to reduce future vulnerability. The destruction of unsafe infrastructure and buildings can provide an opportunity for rebuilding with better standards, or relocation to a better place if the present site is found specifically vulnerable. Particularly damaging disasters will also focus on relief aid and rehabilitation investment, thus, providing developmental opportunities that were previously unavailable. Damaged buildings may highlight structural weaknesses, which could be rectified and may serve to improve building and planning regulations.

The 'connect' between population growth, poverty and development is strong and complex. When assessed in terms of the Gross Domestic

Product (GDP) in the context of our large population we are far behind many of the countries of the world. Conditions of poverty, as we have mentioned, often contribute to greater vulnerability of some sections of a population to an environmental disaster. Food insecurity, lack of means of livelihood and capacity to access resources characterise their lives even in normal times.

While the challenge is equally present in rural and urban areas, it is worse in the case of the latter.

Adequate linkages between disasters and development can, for example, reduce the vulnerability of coastal communities to natural hazards by establishing a regional early warning system; applying construction setbacks, greenbelts and other no-build areas; promote early resettlement with provision for safe housing; debris clearance; potable water, sanitation and drainage services and access to sustainable livelihood options; enhance the ability of the natural system to act as a bioshield to protect people and restoring wetlands, mangroves, spawning areas, sea grass beds and coral reefs, and by seeking alternative building design that is cost-effective, appropriate and consistent. It has to be seen as to how the interlinkages between disasters and development could be incorporated in the disaster recovery plan. Rehabilitation and reconstruction phase is the most opportune time to rebuild infrastructure, resources and communities. Recovery plan should encompass the issues related to negative impact of disasters on socio-economic system and the ways and means through which these challenges could be converted into developmental opportunities. We have moved on from post-disaster assistance to pre-disaster preparedness; from readiness to mitigation; from individual aid to restoration of services; and from relief to rehabilitation. A broad disaster recovery plan should include comprehensive sub-plans on:

- Health and Medical Care;
- Creation of Livelihood Options;
- Environmental Protection; and
- Rehabilitation and Reconstruction.

Many endeavours to strengthen the process of recovery need to be taken note of over here. These aim at using modern technology, community participation and assistance from national and international agencies in disaster recovery. The National Institute of Oceanography

(NIO) in Goa has developed a real-time reporting and Internet-accessible coastal sea-level monitoring system. It has been operational at Verem Jetty on the Mandovi River in Goa since September 24, 2005. The gauge uses a cellular modem to put on the Internet real-time sea-level data, which can be accessed by authorised personnel. By using a cellular phone network, coastal sea-level changes are continuously updated on to a web-server. The sea-level gauge website can be made available to television channels to broadcast real-time visualisation of the coastal sea level (Prabhudesai and Joseph, 2006).

An improved Seismographic Network, a network of real-time sea-level gauges in the Indian Ocean and deep-sea pressure sensors has been proposed, along with National Tsunami Warning Centres (NTWCs), for a reliable warning and mitigation network for the region. While satellite communication is expensive, wireless communication infrastructure and the presence of cellular phones have made cellular communication affordable. The sea-level network in the Indian Ocean has been upgraded with the establishment of 23 real-time stations, which form a part of the Global Sea Level Observation System (GLOSS) set up in 1985 and transmit data every hour through the Global Telecommunication System (GTS) of the World Meteorological Organisation (WMO). Deep-ocean Assessment and Reporting of Tsunamis (DART) is another effort. It is a second-generation DART system (DART-II) that is under development. It will allow bi-directional communication, which would enable transmission of tsunami data on demand. This would ensure the measurement and reporting of tsunamis with wave amplitude below the automatic reporting threshold (Prabhudesai and Joseph, *op.cit.*). After the Tsunami, the India Meteorological Department (IMD) has upgraded the existing seismological observatory at Port Blair with a state-of-the-art broadband seismograph system. A network of five temporary field observatories has been established. Permanent observatories have also been planned for some areas. Setting up bio-shields, knowledge centres and agronomic rehabilitation have been called for (Parsai, 2006).

The advancement in science and technology could be used with advantage for speedy long-term recovery. These efforts have been supplemented by international developments in terms of various environmental treaties, international consortiums, sustainable data forums and declarations such as ProVention Consortium, Fribourg Forum, Hemispheric Conference, South Asian Livelihood Options Project etc. The International Decade for Natural Disaster Reduction (IDNDR) helped raise the profile of discussions surrounding the social and economic causes of disasters and acknowledged the mitigation of losses through technological and engineering solutions. Yokohama Strategy in May 1994 endorsed these objectives and further underlined the link between disaster reduction and sustainable development.

The International Strategy for Disaster Risk Reduction aims at carrying the good work ahead. The Strategy aims at: increasing public awareness of the risks that natural, technological, and environmental hazards; obtaining commitment by public authorities to reduce risks to people, their livelihoods, social and economic infrastructure and environmental resources; engaging public participation at all levels of implementation to create disaster- resistant communities through increased partnership and expanded risk reduction networks at all levels; and reducing the economic and social losses of disasters as measured. The World Health Organisation (WHO) Meet in Bangkok in December 2005 aimed at identifying gaps in addressing response, preparedness and recovery for health needs of the affected. One of the major objectives of the Meet was to develop benchmarks and corresponding course of action (The *Hindu,* Dec.28, 2005).

Disaster management is acquiring a global connotation. Besides the United Nations and the World Bank, many international organisations such as Caritas India, Lutheran World Service, Asian Development Bank, Intermediate Technology Development Group (ITDG), Danish International Development Agency, Swedish International Development Agency, Cooperative for Assistance and Relief Everywhere (CARE), International Federation of Red Cross and Red Crescent Societies, Oxfam, etc., are doing substantial work in the area of disaster management.

Of late, the Narmada Bachao Andolan has been drawing attention to the travails of Project Affected People (PAPs), as a result of unthoughtful and insensitive development and rehabilitation policies of the governments. The Andolan has been focusing on issues such as non-compliance with rules, violation of human rights, hardship of the poor etc. One viewpoint is that those who equate development with huge shopping malls, big dams, vehicular proliferation, and global merchandise are never faulted for the negative consequences of development that ignores norms of equity, environmental protection and social justice (Iyer, 2006). We would though not like to go into the debate on utility of the mega projects over here. Yet, the issue to ponder over is that if in normal times, a development project can cause so much displacement and inadequate rehabilitation of PAPs, can we expect a comprehensive rehabilitation policy for natural disasters? The Disaster Management Act 2005 has been passed in India. The Act aims at speedy handling of natural and man-made disasters. It makes way for the setting up of a National Disaster Management Authority at the Central level and a State Disaster Management Authority at the State level. How far and how much it would achieve are questions only time will answer. Meanwhile, the National Disaster Management Authority is already functional and so also are the State Disaster Management Authorities in Orissa and Gujarat.

The Bureau of Indian Standards (BIS) has also initiated several pre-disaster mitigation projects to reduce the impact of natural disasters on life and property as well as bring down social vulnerabilities. It has undertaken standardisation efforts in the area of earthquake engineering. Some new earthquake-resistance techniques have been developed that can be kept in view. One of them is the Base Isolation Technology. It aims at reducing the forces transmitted to the building from the ground by placing the building atop a mechanical system of isolators, sliders and dampers called Base Isolation Technology. Such technologies along with Diagonal Bracing, disaster resistant pier systems, Welded Wire Fabric Reinforcement could help in disaster-resistant construction. Disaster management has been incorporated in the training curricula of All India Services with effect from 2004-05. There is a separate Faculty for disaster management in 29 State Level Administrative Training Institutes. National Council for Educational Research and Training (NCERT) books now include a chapter on disaster management for school children. The All India Council for Technical Education has been advised to include engineering aspects of disaster management in engineering courses. This education and training impetus has to be sustained through informed people's participation. A simple philosophy for coping with disasters is one of government and people working together in a coordinated way, by means of a coherent disaster management system. A Rehabilitation-Reconstruction-Tracking Matrix is being produced that provides salient information on the overall recovery effort. The Matrix brings together information from tsunami-affected countries on what work is being done and what is being planned, who is doing the work, what measurable results are expected, where the work is being done, when the work is expected to begin and end, and its current status, and the source, amount and status of financing etc. The Matrix is at three levels of resolution-regional overview, sector-level status by region and country, and project level status by country. It is expected to provide a comprehensive view of recovery. This Matrix could serve as the platform for coordination of work in the recovery process and its relationship with developmental goals.

There is also a need to strengthen the legal, organisational and procedural objects of disaster management. The Sustainable Disaster Network (SDN) could be a solution. It is a global network of organisations whose mission is to encourage policies, which allow individuals to pursue their goals without intervention. The SDN focuses on the institutional framework within which people act, to ensure that policies encourage individuals to make the best use of resources and protect the environment, while improving both theirs as well as others' well being.

There have been many instances where disasters have hindered development and many more where lopsided development process has led to disasters. Many seismologists now relate earthquakes with high-rise buildings. Dam-induced afflictions such as deforestation, soil erosion, water logging cannot be overlooked. Loss of mangrove plantation in coastal areas has been the cause behind the colossal loss of human lives and property in the intense Tsunami of 2004. The Chennai floods and the inundation of Mumbai in the year 2005 have been the result of faulty and shortsighted urban planning. Disaster recovery is not a one-time isolated exercise. The objectives of rec overy plan canonly be achieved if the conception, execution and evaluation of disaster management programmes are clearly laid down. The interlinkages between all the stages of disaster management cycle as well as between disasters and development have to be recognised and assimilated in the disaster recovery plan.

Q14. Briefly discuss the salient features of the Gujarat earthquake reconstruction programme.

Ans. The salient features of Gujarat earthquake reconstruction programme were as follows:

- The recovery programme was the biggest ever such programme undertaken at that time.
- Multi-hazard resistant reconstruction made mandatory to resist cyclones, earthquake and other natural hazards.
- Guidelines were prepared to direct people for disaster safe construction and repair of houses. Masons training manual was also prepared and over 27000 masons and 6000 engineers were trained for multi-hazard resistant housing reconstruction. Engineers were appointed in villages to supervise housing construction and provide technical guidance.
- Owner driven housing construction facilitated by financial, material and technical assistance by government. Payments were made in three installments for new construction to ensure multi-hazard resistant construction. The second and third installments were given only after verification and certification by engineers.
- Massive information, education and communication activities undertaken to educate people on multi-hazard resistant construction. Over one million pamphlets on safe housing repair and reconstruction distributed in earthquake affected areas.
- Awareness programme about the safe construction practices and retrofitting of houses were shown in 2500 villages. Shake table demonstrations were done for creating awareness among the masses.
- All reconstructed houses are insured against fourteen types of natural and man-made disasters.
- This recovery programme is one of international best practices. For its highly successful implementation of the programme, the GSDMA was awarded the UN SASAKAWA Award, besides several other national and international recognitions.

Q15. Highlight the significance of disaster psycho social care.

Or

What is the importance of disaster psycho social care?

Ans. Psycho-social care in the context of **disasters** refers to comprehensive interventions aimed at addressing a wide range of psychosocial and mental health problems arising in the aftermath of disasters. These interventions help individuals, families and groups to build human capacities, restore social cohesion and infrastructure along with maintaining their independence, dignity and cultural integrity. Psycho-social support helps in reducing the level of actual and perceived stress and in preventing adverse psychological and social consequences amongst disaster-affected community.

Mental health services in disaster interventions are aimed at identification and management of stress related psychological signs and symptoms or mental disorders among disaster-affected persons and persons with pre-existing mental health problems. In addition, psycho-social support interventions are aimed at mental health and psychological well-being, promotion and prevention of psychological and psychiatric symptoms among disaster-affected community.

The Psycho-social care and Mental health services shall be considered as a continuum of the interventions as an important component of general health services in disaster situations. Psycho-social support will comprise of the general interventions related to the larger issues of promoting or protecting psycho-social well-being through relief work, meeting essential needs, restoring social relationships, enhancing coping capacities and promoting harmony among survivors. The mental health services will comprise of interventions aimed at prevention or treatment of psychological and psychiatric symptoms or disorders.

The experience of trauma after any disaster is multidimensional and complex, therefore everyone who is trained in this can make a significant difference in the lives of the affected population. The key goals of adopting a community model of disaster mental health and psycho-social care are:

- Preventing long-term psychiatric disorders in the disaster affected society;
- Providing relief from mental suffering and psychological distress;
- Maintaining mental well-being and equilibrium;
- Promoting positive mental health;
- All the above four become more important for the optimal utilisation of resources and economic opportunities offered

through the community rehabilitation and development programmes (Who, Division of Mental Health, 1991);

- Strengthening the social support networks in the affected area;
- Facilitating the community participation in all activities taken place in mitigation and relief and rehabilitation phase.

Q16. What are the common psychological reactions following a disaster?

Ans. Typically, when someone is faced with the possibility of losing his/her life, loved ones, home and possessions, hopes, dreams and assumptions about life, there will be some degree of psychological impact. This is what usually occurs in the event of a disaster. Disasters of various types are common occurrences throughout the world and have a broad impact on individuals and communities. Despite that, most survivors are able to cope with the effects, rebuild their lives, and recover psychologically. In most cases, the passage of time will lead to the re-establishment of equilibrium. Fundamental to this process is access to public information about normal reactions, personal coping strategies, and when and where to seek help.

First of all one should understand that any psychological and emotional reaction is not itself all negative, for it can increase the chances of the survival of the victim. Stress becomes a threat to mental health when it overwhelms the capacity of the victims to cope with the new situations by mastering their own reactions. A cauldron of emotional reactions can come to boil after a disaster. Although people react differently to traumatic events on the basis of their experiences and personality, there are number of common response that are experienced by the majority of those involved. These common post-disaster reaction include:

- **emotional** (panic attacks, shock, fear, anger, sadness guilt feelings),
- **psychosomatic** (sleep disturbances, physical problems like muscle tension, palpitation, headaches, nausea, diarrhea or constipation, and breathing difficulties),
- **cognitive** (repeated thoughts and involuntarily triggering the memories, nightmares, confusion, flashbacks, difficulty in concentrating and making decisions, memory problems, shortened attention span, etc), and

- **behavioural and attitudinal** (disruptions in social relationship, poor motivation and concentration, lethargy, hopelessness etc) difficulties. Normally, these reactions 'settle' over the first week. If, however, they remain protracted and intense and moreover, If symptoms persist for a period of three months or after that the person is very likely to suffer from various psychological disorders.

Reaction among disaster affected children: Children experience a variety of reactions and feelings in response to a traumatic event or a disaster and require special attention to meet their needs. Children may exhibit behaviors that are not typical for them. For example, an outgoing child may become shy or may revert to a past behavior such as thumb-sucking or baby talk. Since many children lack the verbal and conceptual skills needed to cope effectively with sudden stress, the reactions of their parents and families strongly affect them. In most cases the symptoms will pass after the child has readjusted. When symptoms do continue, it means a more serious emotional problem has developed and the child will need to be referred to a mental health professional

Factors which increase their vulnerability: Children in disasters are often dislocated from their homes, subject to situations which may be difficult and different from their familiar, comfortable and accustomed lives. This along with the death of family members can be considered as the primary source of stress and insecurity in children. However, witnessing hundreds of deaths and injured can result in unhappiness, sadness, fear and worried. Again their and their family members struggle for food, shelter, and other amenities can add to their fear and insecurity and continue to threat their sense of well-being. Witnessing different forms of violence, social unrest and child abuse can also raise their level of vulnerability to the maximum and can have lifetime irreversible impact on their personality. While these factors definitely increase the vulnerability of all children coming in the age range of 1-18 years, we must look at the special vulnerability of some children within this bigger group in a disaster scenario. Their needs get compounded by the pre-disaster living conditions of some children and the new demands of post-disaster living conditions. These unexpected living conditions many a times go beyond their normal coping strategies and their ability to adjust with the new situation. The next section will be devoted to the specific situations of these special groups of affected children in a disaster scenario.

Factors responsible for their reactions: The mental health and psycho-social impact of any disaster on children depends largely on the following factors:

- their developmental age,
- type of disasters (disasters caused by manmade hazards affect children's psyche in a much deeper way, e.g. communal riots and terrorism)
- the nature of loss they experienced,
- the amount of exposure to trauma,
- sufferings/devastation they witnessed,
- social support dynamics prevail during that phase of disaster, and
- the nature of post-disaster care specially designed to meet their multifarious needs.

Psychological and Social effects include:

- Fear, insecurity and anxiety;
- Loss of protected and familiar environment, where children were staying before the disaster. Generally after a disaster there is a drastic change of place of living. It could be in terms of living in a relief camp or temporary shelter or shifting to some other relative's place. This displacement creates tremendous stress in the children.
- Sadness and depression (often difficult to recognize);
- Anger and irritability;
- Behavioural problems like disobeying, argumentative, and aggression, lying, stealing (in later phase if the psycho-social needs are not addressed);
- Performance deterioration (immediate and long-term) in academics other co-curricular activities;
- Difficulty in relationship/friendship, therefore might suffer from loneliness;

- Increased risk of substance abuse like, consuming alcohol, drugs, narcotics etc., and involvement in delinquent activities (for preadolescent and adolescent groups);
- Subsequent personality disorders.

Although the following problems are social and/or educational in nature but certainly have far reaching psychological impact at the individual and community level:

- Family disorganisation, such as death of one parent or both parents or father/mother marries somebody else after the death of the spouse or children were adopted by somebody else;
- Change of life style and Change in social roles. For example, in case of death of earning members and parents, the child has to take the role of the family head, take care of the younger siblings, go to the market, manage the household chores, etc;
- Unaccompanied children: starvation, child trafficking, sexual abuse/witnessing rape and other forms of violence, child labour/exploitation;
- School dropout rate increases tremendously especially for girls.

Apart from the psycho-social effects of disasters, disasters do have adverse physical and educational effects, which compound the reactions of psycho-social effects followed by disasters. However, irrespective of the type and severity of any natural and manmade disaster, it is more important to understand how children who have experienced disaster would be processing the information and what sort of reactions they show as a result of such experiences of disasters. Therefore, it is imperative to understand how children at various ages would be viewing their losses and trauma.

Reaction among disaster affected adolescents: Peer reactions are especially significant in this age group. The adolescent needs to know that his/her fears are both appropriate and shared by others. A disaster may stimulate fear concerning the loss of their family or fear related to their body. The family's need to pull together threatens their natural branching away from them. Disasters disrupt their peer relationships and school life. As children get older, their responses begin to resemble adult reactions to disasters. They may also have a combination of childlike reactions mixed with adult responses. Teenagers may show more risk-taking behaviors than normal (reckless driving, use of drugs, etc.). Teens may feel overwhelmed by their emotions, and may be unable to discuss them with their families.

Reaction among disaster affected adults: Adults are focused on family, home, jobs, and financial security. Many are involved with caring for older parents as well. Pre-disaster life often involves maintaining a precarious balance between competing demands. Following a disaster, this balance is lost, with the introduction of the enormous time, financial, physical, and emotional demands of recovery. Somatic reactions are especially present in those who are less able to experience and express their emotions directly. Cultural, gender-based, or psychological factors may interfere with emotional expression and seeking social support. Anxiety and depression are common, as adults contend with both anxiety about future threats and grief about the loss of home, lifestyle, or community.

Reaction among disaster affected older adults: The impact of disaster-related losses has shown that a higher incidence of personal loss, injury and death are experienced by older adults. In addition, existing problems with sight, hearing and mobility all place older adults at higher risk for physical injury. Research has also shown that older adults are less likely to evacuate, less likely to heed warnings, less likely to acknowledge hazards and dangerous situations, and are much slower to respond to the full impact of losses. A larger proportion of older persons, as compared with younger age groups, have chronic illnesses that may worsen with the stress of a disaster, particularly when recovery extends over months. They are more likely to be taking medications that need to be replaced quickly following a disaster.

Q17. What is community based disaster psycho social care?

Ans. The psycho-social aspects of disasters on human beings have been acknowledged as an international agenda (WHO, 1992). However, in India, the psycho-social aspects have never been emphasized until very recently after tsunami, 2004. The Bhopal gas tragedy (1984) was the most important disaster to draw the national attention due to its severe impact and the sensitivity of the politico-economic issues involved. The psycho-social impact was studied systematically although intervention programmes were more of psychiatric in nature. Latur earthquake (1993), and Andhra Pradesh Super Cyclone (1996) were disasters in which mental health professionals took an active part in terms of providing mental health services and undertaking research to study the psycho-social impact of these disasters.

The ICMR studies over last twenty years have provided strong base for integration of mental health services with general health care services and sensitization of the community members and rescue workers. However, it has been difficult to integrate the mental health services at micro and macro level. Recently, National Disaster Management Agency and National Institute of Disaster Management has mixed experiences in providing health care services in disaster situations. However, the finer details of the mechanisms and strategies for integration of mental health services with general health care services still need to be worked out.

In the post Tsunami phase in India, the WHO along with the Department of Social Welfare, United Nations Team for (UNTRS), and partners have developed a model for providing sustained, low cost community-based volunteer provided support systems. Community level workers who are the anchor for this programme are selected from various categories of people, including teachers, health workers, and members of self help groups etc, who have volunteered for this purpose. A cascading system of training was developed and in Tamil Nadu, 2813 Community Level Workers (CLWs) were trained in the 11 affected Districts. They were able to support more than 30,000 families and 150,000 individuals.

The work of the Community Level Workers (CLWs) was coordinated under the Department of Social Welfare and the District Social Welfare Officers provided coordination, supervision and linkage with health systems. An exclusive cell was created in the Directorate of Social Welfare for management of the entire activity in Tamil Nadu. Similar programmes were taken up in Kerala, Andhra Pradesh and Pondicherry and have proved to be of immense value in providing psycho-social support. Special attention needs to be paid to children and school are a good opportunity to reach them.

There has to be community-based support for those who are out of school. The needs and expectations of the community changes over the period of recovery and rehabilitation and the programme needs to be aligned to this scenario. Alcohol abuse are related problems also seem to be prevalent in such settings and the Community Level Workers (CLWs) were provided additional capacity for addressing this important issue. A resource kit has been developed compiling all the materials and manuals and will serve as a guide for disaster preparedness and mitigation programmes.

Role of schools in community (school) based disaster psycho-social care: Impact of major natural and man-made disasters on school children and school buildings have been enormous in last few decades in India. A few incidents, such as, Gujarat earthquake on 26 January 2001 claimed lives of 971 school children and 31 teachers and destroyed/damaged 1884 school buildings and 5950 classrooms; a devastating school fire in Kumbakonam (Tamil Nadu) claimed 94 lives of young children on 16 July 2004, 17,000 children died and 2,448 schools collapsed in the 2005 Kashmir earthquake; 441 school children died in a stampede at a school function in Dabwali (Haryana) in December 1995. All these incidents invoke tremendous stress and other psychological reactions amongst the children teachers and others in the schools.

After Gujarat earthquake, riots, Tsunami in South India, earthquake in J &K, training of teachers in basic disaster psycho-social care skills have been done successfully and a large number of teachers are now trained in this aspect. It was found that training of teachers in basic psycho-social care skills was helpful to the teachers to help themselves, their family members, colleagues, staff, children and the community at large. They considered it as a part of the basic survivor's skills or life competency skills that every teacher must learn.

Life Competency Skills for Teachers :

Try and Understand the children	Reduce the impact of the disaster on them	Give them care and support
Serve their behaviour and listen to what they say	Listen to what they say	Use play to offer support and help
Accept their behaviour and what they say completely	Give them love and assurance and meet their basic needs	Talk with the children and find out what they need
Continuously monitor what they say to you and how they behave	Model positive living and good coping skills	Try to help them to return to their normal life routines

School teachers: Training and retraining teachers on these life competency skills would not only help them to identify children with stress symptoms, behavioural and emotional problems but also to understand the performance deterioration of disaster affected children in better way. However, they are trained; they should try to follow the dos and don'ts mentioned below.

Do's & Don'ts

- Help the child talk about the issue and note behaviours/reactions.
- Give extra attention to new children in your class make them comfortable.
- Reassure the child.
- Monitor the academic progress.
- Provide extra academic support to cope with the academic loss.
- Listen to these children with patience.
- Enhance the self-esteem of children.
- Keep interacting with the family.
- Maintaining the contact and discussion with the community level psychosocial workers.
- Keeping a record of abnormal reactions and behavioural problems found among the target group i.e. the disaster victims.
- Observe disaster affected children and their behaviour pattern to notice any change in their behaviour and habit.
- Do not ridicule the child for regressive behaviours.
- Do not say that everybody faced same difficulties/losses, so try to be normal.
- Do not scold child in front of other children in classroom in case the child is not able to perform (as compared to his pre-disaster performance), do class works.
- Don't say that you have become careless and do not want to study in the pretext/excuse of disaster.
- Don't say that you try to forget the incident, everything will be normal as before.

- Do not give false promise.

Thus, the role of schools/teachers in providing psycho-social support to the disaster affected people inside and outside the school community has been significant in India. Therefore, the forthcoming National Guidelines on Psycho-social Care and Mental Health Services in Disasters in India has included capacity building of teachers in these skills as a crucial step, which would be institutionalized shortly. Teachers are also considered as an important group of Community Level Workers (CLWs) to provide psycho-social care services to the disaster affected population.

As teachers in a caregiver's role they must understand the process and procedures of facilitating children's fast recovery from the trauma. This will enable the children to withstand the negative effects of the catastrophic event in a more appropriate way. Here the adult caregivers can be divided into 4 prime categories viz. parents/relatives, school teachers, and caregivers from outside. especially pediatricians. These caregivers must understand the emotional/behaviour reactions the child is exhibiting and then offer support and security to the child. They also are responsible to develop healthy coping mechanisms in the child.

Peer as counsellors: Since, school based disaster management is now being made a compulsory safety practice in all schools and this involves various groups of children from the planning to the implementation stage, little orientation on the psychological impact of disasters to these groups would work wonder. Peer counseling formally or informally takes place amongst/between children in every school. Traumatized children often feel comfortable and convenient to share their feelings, thoughts, emotions and behaviours with their friends, seniors, or even with juniors. After any disaster if teachers orient the children in classrooms to follow certain dos and don'ts mentioned below, then teachers can monitor the child's all round progress very easily. This would help them to know about these traumatized children easily.

Q18. Write down the do's and don'ts in disaster psycho social care.

Ans. While interacting/providing psycho-social counseling to the disaster affected population, the following tips would provide some guidance:

Day say

- These are normal reactions to abnormal situations.

- I can understand that you feel this way.
- It was not your fault.
- You are not mad.
- Things may never be same as it before the incident.

Do not say

- It could have been worse.
- You can always have another house and car.
- It is best if you stay busy.
- Leave everything to God.
- You try control your emotions.
- This has happened to others also, so you need not behave in this way.
- Try to forget about the disaster.
- As a counselor in a community one can:
- Encourage the clients to resume his daily chores and occupational activities at the earliest,
- Encourage them to express and ventilate,
- Allow and encourage them to perform the rites and rituals,
- Guide them to avoid indiscriminate use of tranquilizers,
- Be careful of any addiction that may clients may opt,
- Provide empathetic assurance,
- Encourage them to attend religious discourse, spirituality camps, meditation camps, etc,
- Request them to ask for help when they feel bad continuously and assure them that asking help is not a sign of weakness or of madness,
- Encourage them to speak to others, share feelings even if they are strange, absurd and silly,
- Take one task at a time,
- delegate responsibility,
- Consult a psychologist or psychiatrist before taking any medication to get relief from the symptoms.

QUESTION PAPERS

MSWE-003 : DISASTER MANAGEMENT

June, 2020

Note: (i) Answer all the five questions. (ii) All questions carry equal marks. (iii) Answer to question numbers 1 and 2 should not exceed 600 words each.

Q1. Describe the relationship between hazard, risk, vulnerability and capacity.

Or

Discuss the essential components and the practice of Relief Management in India.

Q2. Explain the differential impact of disaster on men and women.

Or

Examine the relevance of a common damage assessment format.

Q3. Answer any two of the following questions in about 300 words each:

(a) What is drought? Briefly discuss its types and causes.

(b) Describe the process involved in mitigation.

(c) Discuss the basic features of ICs.

(d) Explain various Biological Disorders.

Q4. Answer any four of the following questions in about 150 words each:

(a) What is the difference between task force and strike team?

(b) Explain disaster release model.

(c) Discuss the role of community in disaster management.

(d) Differentiate between forecast and warning.

(e) Why is triage done in case of mass causality incidents?

(f) Enlist the important aspects of pre-disaster recovery plan.

Q5. Write short notes on any five of the following in about 100 words each:

(a) Landslides

(b) Forest fires

(c) Steps in hazard identification and risk assessment

(d) Components of recovery

(e) Common psychological reactions following a disaster

(f) Incident command system

(g) Mandate of NDMA

(h) Community contingency fund

❑❑❑

Happy moments,
Praise God.
Difficult moments,
Seek God.
Quiet moments,
Worship God.
Painful moments,
Trust God.
Every moment,
Thank God.

MSWE-003 : DISASTER MANAGEMENT

December, 2020

Note: Attempt any five questions. All questions carry equal marks. Answer to question no. 1 and 2 should not exceed 600 words each.

Q1. Describe the relationship between hazard, vulnerability, risk and capacity.

Or

Discuss various preparedness and mitigation measures for combating man-made disasters.

Q2. Identify the organizations for managing disasters at the national, state and district levels.

Or

Describe the components of community-based disaster management.

Q3. Answer any two of the following questions in about 300 words each:

(a) Discuss the concept, types, causes and impact of drought.

(b) Highlight the various types of mitigation process.

(c) Explain the importance of gender in the management of disasters.

(d) Describe the main features of the ECLAC methodology for assessment.

Q4. Answer any four of the following questions in about 150 words each:

(a) Explain the concept of an end to end early warning system.

(b) What is the importance of coordination in relief management?

(c) How does GIS help in preventing epidemics?

(d) Write three criteria for successful mass casualty management.

(e) What are the primary Incident Command System (ICS) functions?

(f) What are the important features of a disaster recovery plan?

Q5. Write short notes on any five of the following in about 100 words each:

(a) Disaster

(b) Disaster release model

(c) Earthquake risk mitigation strategy

(d) Stampede

(e) Bhopal gas leak

(f) Types of mitigation

(g) Unified command

(h) Triage

❑❑❑

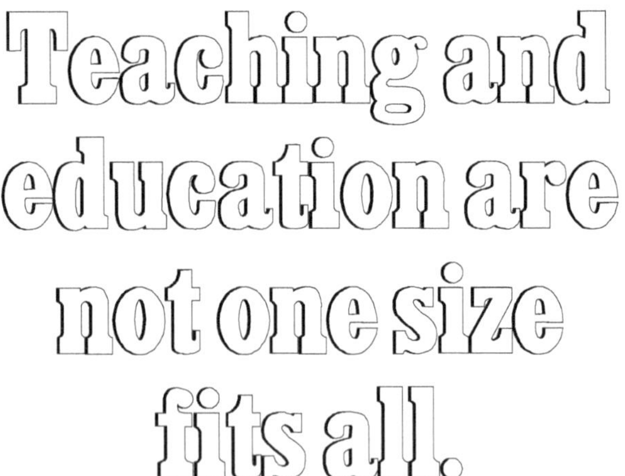

MSWE-003 : DISASTER MANAGEMENT

June, 2021

Note: Answer all the five questions. All questions carry equal marks. Answers to questions no. 1 and 2 should not exceed 600 words each.

Q1. Describe the relationship between hazard, vulnerability, risk and capacity.

Or

Explain the meaning and need of Community-based Disaster Management.

Q2. Discuss the process and practice of managing relief commodities and services.

Or

Examine the relevance of a common damage assessment format.

Q3. Answer any two of the following questions in about 300 words each:

(a) Describe different types of disasters.

(b) Explain the concept and four components of an End-to-End Warning System.

(c) Discuss the process of disaster recovery planning.

(d) Elucidate the principles and approaches for post-disaster recovery.

Q4. Answer any four of the following questions in about 150 words each:

(a) What was the idea behind the proclamation of IDNDR?

(b) Briefly describe the process involved in mitigation.

(c) State the main causes of epidemics after natural disasters.

(d) What is the difference between three types of triage?

(e) How would you assess the affected population in a disaster?

(f) Discuss the important aspects of pre-disaster recovery plan.

Q5. Write short notes on any five of the following in about 100 words each:

(a) Disaster

(b) Do's and Don'ts for man-made disaster emergencies

(c) Vulnerability of women and men in disasters

(d) Health services in disasters

(e) Incident Command System

(f) Disaster Management Cycle

(g) Community-based disaster psycho-social care

(h) Disaster Crunch Model

❑❑❑

Education's purpose is to replace an empty mind with an open one.

MSWE-003 : DISASTER MANAGEMENT

December, 2021

Note: (i) Answer all the five questions. (ii) All questions carry equal marks. (iii) Answer to question numbers 1 and 2 should not exceed 600 words each.

Q1. Describe various models of disaster management.

Or

Explain the way relief is managed in India along with various tools available for the purpose.

Q2. Discuss the factors affecting disaster recovery process.

Or

Discuss the common psycho-social reactions found among the disaster survivors.

Q3. Answer any two of the following questions in about 300 words each:

(a) Explain the salient features of man-made disasters.

(b) Describe the components of community based disaster management.

(c) What is Incident Command System (ICS) and why is it useful?

(d) What are the stages of post-disaster management? Name the major activities in each stage.

Q4. Answer any four of the following questions in about 150 words each:

(a) List the major initiatives taken by India during IDNDR for disaster risk reduction.

(b) What is the difference between a forecast and warning?

(c) Briefly explain the concept and goals of mitigation.

(d) How does GIS help in preventing epidemics?

(e) Define damage assessment and list the objectives of assessment.

(f) Enlist the steps in hazard identification and risk assessment.

Q5. Write short notes on any five of the following in about 100 words each:

(a) Nuclear disaster

(b) Importance of gender in the management of disasters

(c) Disaster health care management

(d) ECLAC method

(e) Disaster recovery plan

(f) Components of disaster recovery

(g) Do's and Don'ts in disaster psychosocial care

(h) Triage

❑❑❑

EDUCATION
is not the learning of facts,
but the training of the
mind to think.

MSWE-003 : DISASTER MANAGEMENT

June, 2022

Note: Answer all the five questions. All questions carry equal marks. Answers to questions no. 1 and 2 should not exceed 600 words each.

Q1. Define Disaster. Describe different types of disasters with examples.

Or

Describe the concept of an End-to-End Early Warning System. Provide an overview of early warning system for cyclones in India.

Q2. Explain the differential vulnerability of women and men to disaster.

Or

Discuss the ways relief is managed in India. Explain various tools for managing relief.

Q3. Answer any two of the following questions in about 300 words each:

(a) Describe the implications of chemical and biological disasters.

(b) Explain the meaning and need of community-based disaster management.

(c) What is Incident Command System (ICS) and why is it useful?

(d) Define damage assessment and list the objectives of assessment.

Q4. Answer any four of the following questions in about 150 words each:

(a) Explain various tools that can be used for hazard analysis.

(b) Briefly describe the process involved in mitigation.

(c) What are the main causes of epidemics after natural disasters?

(d) List the factors affecting disaster recovery process.

(e) Explain the concept of disaster management cycle.

(f) State the significance of disaster psycho-social care.

Q5. Write short notes on any five of the following in about 100 words each:

(a) Disaster Pressure and Release Model

(b) Landslide risk mitigation strategy

(c) Sources of chemical disasters

(d) Difference between forecast and warning

(e) Pre-disaster management

(f) Common reactions among disaster affected children

(g) Triage

(h) Calamity Relief Fund (CRF)

❑❑❑

"Education is not the learning of facts, but the training of the mind to think."

Albert Einstein

www.ingramcontent.com/pod-product-compliance
Ingram Content Group UK Ltd.
Pitfield, Milton Keynes, MK11 3LW, UK
UKHW021702190726
13853UKWH00001B/402

9 789390 479740